Echoes

Teachings from the Past
Wisdom for the Present

Debra Skelton

Foreword by Brian Robertson and Simon James

Tellwell Talent

www.tellwell.ca

ISBN

978-1-77302-767-8 (Hardcover)

978-1-77302-771-5 (Paperback)

978-1-77302-769-2 (eBook)

*Dedicated to the pioneering community, past and present,
of the Open Door Sanctuary*

Acknowledgements

I gratefully acknowledge the generosity and support of
Reverend Brian Robertson, Reverend Simon James,
Reverend Terri Woolgar, Deborah Davis, Lorna Lyons,
Linda Muir, Philippe Szpirglas, Jacqueline Weill
and her daughters, and Beverly Stokes.

*This book is offered in gratitude to a woman of
faith and courage - my mother, Kathleen.*

INNER QUEST PRESS

Foreword

The captivating passages within this book reveal a "lost" wisdom tradition: that of Spiritualism.

For many years, not only the names but the philosophical outpourings of these remarkable individuals have been lost to history. Now, in some cases for the first time in over 100 years, the inspiration of the Spirit as it touched these men and woman in a time of change and radicalism is brought together for the modern reader.

At long last the words of many of the great minds of Spiritualism rank here alongside those of the world's revered wisdom traditions.

Debra Skelton has prepared a feast for the spiritually hungry of the heart and mind.

Enjoy.

Brian Robertson and Simon James

Table of Contents

List of Authors

Barbanell , Maurice
Blake, Frank T.
Cadwallader, Mary E.
Carey, Alice
Coleman, Lewis S.
Colville, W.J.
Davis, Andrew Jackson
Doten, Lizzie
Edwards, Harry
Evans, W.H.
Findlay, Arthur
Ford, Will
Hardinge Britten, Emma
Higginson, Gordon
Hugo, Victor
Hull, Mattie E.
Kitson, Alfred
Korretyr
Leaf, Horace
Leonard, John C.
Longfellow, Henry Wadsworth
Love, Adelaide
Marryat, Florence
Massey, Gerald
Maynard, Nettie Colburn

Miller, Paul
Morse, J.J.
Owen, Robert Dale
Peebles, J.M.
Richmond, Cora V. Hatch
Robertson, James
Savage, Minot
Schlesinger, Julia
Spear, J. Murray
Stead, William Thomas
Swaffer, Hannen
Swedenborg, Emanuel
Tuttle, Hudson & Emma Rood
Wallis, M.H. and E.W.
Waterman, Nixon
Watson, Elizabeth Lowe
White, Nellie R.
Wilcox, Ella Wheeler
Woodhull, Victoria
Yeats, W.B.

Introduction

"Lives of great men all remind us,
We can make our lives sublime,
And, departing, leave behind us
Footprints on the sands of time."

Henry Wadsworth Longfellow

Any philosophy, however graceful, must be of benefit to oneself or one's fellow creatures. If not, it remains an interesting but fruitless pursuit. The inspired wisdom of countless philosophers and activists of the past is abundantly rich in practical knowledge for the modern world. However, much of what they had to say remains unread and unheard. The modern mind often finds it difficult to understand the archaic language of our ancestors and their precious books sadly gather dust on the shelves of libraries the world over.

For this reason I humbly offer the spiritual seeker this contemporary anthology, a highly readable glimpse into the minds and passions of those spiritual seekers who came before us. I hope that a new generation may once again be touched by the startling relevance of their wisdom for today's world.

Echoes gives voice to some of the great philosophers within our theurgic lineage. This edition focuses on those of our ancestors who found inspiration within the spiritual renaissance of the 19th century and the modern Spiritualist movement.

Within these pages you will find an abridged and, I trust, respect-fully edited selection of passages by those philosophers who put their understanding into action and thereby changed the world. It has been my intention, by modifying some of the language, to make their writings more easily accessible to the modern eye and ear, while maintaining the integrity of their vision. May you be guided by the abundant riches contained herein and benefit from the depth of their experience.

It is sincerely hoped that the echo of these voices from the past may bring a sense of easement to those who grieve, understanding to those who suffer, and upliftment to all.

Debra Skelton

PART ONE: THE INSPIRERS

M.H. and E.W. Wallis

Minnie Harriot Wallis
1854-unknown
and
Edward Walter Wallis
1855-1914
British Mediums, Inspirational Speakers
Publishers: *The Two Worlds*

M.H. and E.W. Wallis

Awakening

Be Thyself

From Spirit to Spirit

Death's Chiefest Surprise

No Unknowing

Respectful Conditions

Listen

Letter to My Friends

Awakening

To every individual, life affords just what one is prepared to get from it. One finds what one seeks. So much depends upon possessing the seeing eye, the listening ear and the understanding heart as to whether we go through life poor or rich in spirit. The prime fact is our inner consciousness. What we feel, think, know, enjoy, suffer, love and struggle to attain constitutes our world – the thought-world in which we live.

Life is not a result of blind chance. There is no accident or failure. The universe is under the dominion of Mind, or Intelligence, guided and ordered to a purposed end – a process rather than a final manifestation. In the human being, the power that is infinite is individualized and attaining to self-consciousness.

The origin of humankind so far as the body is concerned is, after all, a minor matter. Whether one sprang from monkeys or from mud is immaterial. The body is not the being and never has been; it is only an agent for one's use. That which is called Life, or Spirit, is as much the soul of the atom, of the blade of grass, of the insect which floats in the summer sunshine, as of you; but in you, it attains personal consciousness. You, the spirit, can trace your heredity beyond the monkey and the protoplasmic slime, to God. You have descended from, and are ever related to, the Infinite Spirit.

Be Thyself

The thoughts and feelings we create determine what we shall become. The power for self-expression and self-realization rests and abides within us. These are the keynotes of spiritual understanding. We do not deny that environments hamper and limit, that education and misdirection bind and enslave. We admit that our heredity counts for a great deal. But we do say that the prime factor amid all circumstances is oneself.

The building of character, consciously and purposely, is no easy task, and is one that is too seldom fully undertaken. I speak of following one's highest ideals of right, honour and truth, overcoming bias and prejudice, and rendering loving service to others. It will be in this direction that the greatest progress will be made in the evolution of true and upstanding manhood and womanhood.

A new attitude is being assumed by ourselves towards ourselves. The old cringing and self-deprecatory, "I cannot" conceptions are rapidly passing away and the affirmation that we are spiritual beings, progressive and responsible, is taking its place. The knowledge is sending us faring forth with confident spirits to learn to use our thought power and express our true nature. We now realize, as never before, the operation of the great law of consequences: that we reap what we sow both here and hereafter, and that reform must begin in the individual.

While improvement of environments and the breaking down of limitations will exert a beneficial influence and afford opportunity to the one who is ready to advance, the real and permanent upward trend will only be revealed when the soul-self is awakened, and dominates as a moving force in the ordering of life.

"Be thyself" is written in the very principles of our being. We have too long looked for salvation and liberation to be accomplished for us, not by us. "Believe and be saved" has been dinned into us until we have failed to realize that we must trust and exercise the potency of our own spirits, the divine life dwelling within us, and act as if we really, honestly and fully believe that we are creatures of the living God.

We have sold our spiritual heritage for a mess of potage far too long and have supinely bent our backs to the enslavers. But the time is drawing near when we shall be free. There is no miracle-worker like this wonderful and rational faith in the soul; no liberator like the love of all that is true, pure, good and beautiful; no redeemer so powerful as knowledge rightly applied; no gospel that can equal the realization of our innate divinity, our immortal heritage, our inherent capacity to understand and the attunement of ourselves to the principles of life.

The fact that the individual is a centre of deific possibilities implies the innate divinity of every human being. Every person is related to and dependent upon the Supreme Life. The radiations from the Infinite Mind circulate throughout the universe and we are continually bathing in the atmosphere of divine love, breathing it in unconsciously.

And the aura of the All Good touches us at all points.

From Spirit to Spirit

Use and beauty are inseparable. All science, art and religion are but the broken utterances of your spirit attempting to read the riddle of the universe and to understand your own relation to Spirit. The object of all the experiences through which you pass in the earthly pilgrimage is the deepening of your individual consciousness, until there is an awakening from within. You then become aware of your spiritual nature and exercise your powers in harmony with the principles which govern all expressions of the Divine Life; until the meaning is revealed and passes from Spirit to spirit, from God to you.

The message which God speaks to you, and you to God, is ever from Spirit to spirit. This experience comes sooner or later, here or hereafter, to every individual. It may come as the result of a bitter trial, a disappointment, a great grief or bereavement, or as an awakening from within to a sense of unity with the Divine. It may not be enjoyed all the time, for the things of the sense-world drag us down; but the still small voice of the spirit persistently calls us to gain that state in which the spirit realizes its harmony with all Life.

The Infinite Mind is the divine reasoner, is reason itself. Those who are psychically gifted do not reason things out by process of logic; they rather feel or apprehend. There is thrown upon their consciousness the picture of the thing they intuitively realize; and it is this which is, in reality, the discerning of spiritual things. They think and know in feelings and revelations, by direct perception rather than by process of reasoning.

To many, this state of consciousness may seem impossible to comprehend, but that is always the case; someone who dwells on one plane is out of touch with someone who dwells on another. Two persons may sit side by side in an audience and listen to the same words, and yet that which is spoken will appeal to each in an entirely different manner because they are on different planes. Every individual is what and where they are as a result of their life and experience, and each state is part of the process of their education. The deepest and most intimate relations are those where community of interest exists – where thought answers thought, where love responds to love without words, and the communion is from spirit to spirit.

The individual who loses faith in himself will lose faith in others. Faith in the divine Self within and the divine Universal Life is vital. It cannot be argued about, explained or proven by reason. It can be felt, that is all. One who has once realized it has had a vision of the Great Reality, has breathed the divine air of the Eternal Life, and dwells in perfect serenity.

Death's Chiefest Surprise

All forms and organisms are due to an energy, which energy we call life or spirit. So, it is spirit first, body afterwards; spirit the cause, body the effect.

Every birth is a materialization of the spirit impulse and the result of spirit activity. There is, between the external and the internal body, an intermediate link and that is called the soul or spirit body. That spirit body is the agent by means of which all thought, consciousness, affection and volition can be expressed.

The body does not live. It is merely vitalized by the spiritual body. The eye does not see. The ear does not hear. They are but the appropriate instruments, vitalized by the interpenetrating spirit-body. It is the spiritual ear or the spiritual eye which enables the indwelling spirit to receive impressions and discover the purposes of being. It is the spirit body that causes the development of the physical body, expressing itself through it.

The process of death is but the casting off of the garment of clay, so that the interior spiritual body may be far more actively employed by the Spirit in the process of consciousness upon a more subtle plane.

The spirit world is a great thought-world. There, thoughts become things. Your mental life affects the substances of that world. The great surprise is that you cannot get away from yourself.

It is death which introduces you to your true state; for death is the unmasking time in the masquerade of life. In the spirit world, it is our *motives* that are taken into account. Thoughts may be veiled and motives may be hidden on this side of life; but in the next world, each one of us is seen as we are, and perhaps this is the chiefest surprise.

One of the greatest regrets of those who pass out of this life is, "Oh, if only I had known, I would have done so differently." The great claim of Modern Spiritualism upon you may be expressed in the words, "*Now* is the accepted time." Now is the time for you to let the good thought flow out into action, and by your example and influence, to help others and stimulate them, to make the pathway freer for them.

By reminding you that you are three-fold in your nature – body, soul and spirit – possessing those powers of the soul by means of which you may see, hear and come into relationship with the spirit-side of your nature, Spiritualism has given to the world a light which will shine into the dark places.

No Unknowing

The intense joy which results from the realization of the actual presence of the so-called dead – of their independent activity and of their unchanged nature and affection; that they are truly alive, thinking, remembering, loving and happy; that they are just themselves – must be experienced to be understood. Let some talk as they may about the superiority of those who believe without such evidences. Even they themselves are thrilled and delighted when they receive actual and satisfactory demonstrations of the personal survival of their own loved ones. We know of no means whereby such evidences can be obtained save through mediumship. When once the conviction has been driven home, and the truth of spirit has been realized, nothing can destroy it.

The Spiritualist stands upon firm ground. One knows that intercourse between the two worlds is real. For in the light of the demonstrated evidences of continued conscious existence after death, it is clear that the human being is, even now, a spirit served by organs.

Consequently, the basis of all religious experience is the spiritual consciousness of the human being. There could be no revelation to you of spiritual truth if you were not a spirit possessing the capabilities of receiving and comprehending, of interpreting and applying, the revelations and inspirations which quicken the inner self.

Spiritualism is the science, philosophy and religion of life. It points us to life, not death. Spiritual gifts must be coveted and cultivated so that the worship of God may find expression in those loving services rendered, in both worlds.

Respectful Conditions

I once made an appointment to attend a séance. As the time grew near I dawdled about, disinclined to go. At last, disliking to break my promise, I hurried off. Afterwards I wished I had never entered the place, for the moment I stepped into the room the influence seemed to stifle me. Contention, jealousy and ill-feeling existed between the people present, and a most miserable time we had of it.

The manifestations of spirit friends and the expression of their thoughts depend, to a very great extent, on the conditions we supply to them. The prerequisite for success is a generous frame of mind. If mediums are at ease, and not surrounded by cynics who distrust or condemn them, there will be the best results. I think, too, that pure motives and unselfish actions by honest, single-minded workers, in the body or out of it, are ever likely to exert an inspiring and beneficial influence.

The great work before us is to try to understand the subtle laws and forces employed by the spirit world in their efforts. I believe we sometimes mix ourselves into their work and hinder rather than help. We need more patience, more study, more facts, more observations impartially made and fewer generalizations. Spirits are entitled to our respect and gratitude for their efforts on our behalf.

Listen

Helen Keller, the blind deaf mute, won her way to college but realized the disadvantages of that institution after she got there.

She said, "I used to have time to think, to reflect, my mind and I. We would sit together of an evening and listen to the inner melodies of the spirit which one hears only in leisure moments. But in college, there is no time to commune with one's thoughts. One goes to college to learn, not to think, it seems. When one enters the portals of learning, one leaves behind the dearest pleasures – solitude, books and imagination, outside with the whispering pines and the sunlit odourous woods."

We must have time to listen, to see, to understand and respond. We need not wonder that many people are going into the silence to gain insight, strength and serenity. With unrest, anxiety and sensationalism, the mind becomes disturbed and, like water stirred from its depths and broken into waves upon the surface, it cannot reflect the blue heavens. It can only give back broken gleams of truth.

The phenomena connected with the subtle domain where mind and matter meet, require the most unerring discernment and intuition for their correct interpretation. The seen and the unseen worlds are so intimately related that every earnest and sincere effort put forth on this side for self-control and expression, and for the good of others, relates us to like-minded people on the other side who are, by our aspirations, enabled to respond with helpful influences. The more fully this is realized by us, the greater will be the assistance and inspiration that we shall receive.

In order to know more, you must be more. Faith strikes its roots deep in the spirit, and often intuition is a safer guide than reason. When, by constant practice, one has so quickened the spiritual perceptions that one can receive conscious impressions from invisible attendants, one will never be without counsellors.

The spirit world is not so distant as it seems and the veil of materiality which hides it from our view, by untiring aspiration, can be rent in twain. We only need to listen earnestly and attentively and we shall soon learn to keep step to the music of the upper spheres.

However, the development of mediumistic sensitiveness, and the cultivation of the psychical powers of clairvoyant perception, should not be allowed to dominate one's thoughts or occupy all one's time. It must be remembered that life has its daily duties, its ordinary relationships, and practical responsibilities. The true development is the harmonious all-round cultivation and exercise of all one's powers, the bringing out and enjoying of all one's capabilities – physically, mentally, morally and spiritually. The cultivation of psychic power is not everything. The development of sensitiveness should be desired as a means to an end, rather than the end-all and be-all of life.

Communion with departed loved ones and psychic development will fail to produce their legitimate effects if, while they comfort, enlighten and inspire us, they do not deepen our convictions, broaden our sympathies, and kindle a light in the inner sanctuary of our consciousness, which will enable us to work and live more wisely and lovingly.

If we mistrust ourselves, we shall want a faith in the Spirit Divine; for no one can truly trust in God who has no faith in oneself, and fails to realize that the fountainhead of power, of growth, of manifestation, is within.

Spiritualism helps us to understand the unity of the spirit and the unity of humankind, in the divine relationship wherein the greatest among us is the servant of all.

The possession of intuitive abilities is an added responsibility. We are only stewards of our powers on behalf of others. Our desire to gain knowledge and influence should be vitalized and dignified by the intention to use them to help, teach and serve our fellows. In such service, we shall ourselves be blessed.

Letter to My Friends

The knowledge that I am a spirit, immortal, and son of God fills me with joy, and a sense of responsibility too. Life is so real and earnest, its duties so many, that I feel almost afraid. But the knowledge that perfection awaits me hereafter if I keep on trying, nerves me to try again, and cheerfully hope and work for the truth and for humanity, making the best of the present hour with its duties and delights.

I would like to say a word to the many good friends who have trusted, helped and strengthened me in the past. It is this; I have endeavoured, feebly it is true, but to the best of my ability, to be a faithful worker of the spirit world; to be worthy of the mission, worthy of your confidence, esteem, trust and goodwill. Having done my best without hope of praise or fear of punishment, I thank you from the bottom of my heart, and shall endeavour to serve, as long as life lasts, the cause of humanity which is the cause of Spiritualism.

I will conclude with some lines given through me at the close of a discourse in America:

We are each and all another,
We can never stand alone,
And, for pain or wrong afflicted,
We must every one atone.

Let us feel that we are brothers,
That our interests are one;
We shall help each other onward,
And the will of God, be done.

Fraternally and heartily yours,
E.W. Wallis

J.J. Morse

J.J. Morse
1848-1919
British Philosopher, Medium
Inspirational Speaker, Author
Editor: *Lyceum Banner* and *Banner of Light*

J.J. Morse

The Whole Nature

Duty to This World

Sensible Growth

Heart of the Matter

Special Gifts

The Divinity Within

The Whole Nature

Some people seem to think that spirituality is a sort of golden cake that they may take a bite out of and be benefited the same as the eating of manna in the olden times. Nothing of the sort. The spirituality of the individual does not depend upon the cultivation of one special faculty, but upon the entire rounding out of the whole nature, mentally, morally and spiritually.

When this development of character is strong, the individual, self-poised, can rise triumphant over the perplexities of daily life, ride the storms of hatred in safety and emerge at last into a conscious, self-poised existence, fearing no sorrow and dreading no future.

Then there is a spiritual development worthy of the name that is made up of the mental, moral and conscious development of the individual. Such lives have neither time nor inclination to yearn for an especial spiritual development; for they feel the spirituality of their own souls radiating to every part of their being, expressed in every thought and action of their lives.

This is the spiritual development we would suggest to you as being realized in the spirit life. Over there it is not a question of the development of one especial part of a person's nature to make them prominent or noticeable, or to give them some especial grace and quality. One is considered the most spiritual who has the most of spirituality in the *entirety* of one's life, character, thought and action.

Hence then, in spirit, one person may make a point of development in a certain direction; another person's inclination, running into some other channel, may cause them to pursue development in some opposite direction. Yet you could not accuse either of being unspiritual, for they are pursuing the way that seems the proper one for them to pursue; and for them it is, because it seems so to them.

Development in the spiritual world may be intellectual, moral or spiritual; it may be aesthetic, artistic or poetic; it may be the hundred and

Debra Skelton

one different methods of progress and unfoldment. But whatever line of progress may be pursued, the development comes as the natural result of intelligent labour wisely directed.

Duty to This World

We have been consulted over and over again as to the propriety of developing mediumship. We have had to tell many that, as the indications of the possible development of their mediumship were exceedingly small, they had better devote their spare time to doing something serviceable with the powers they possess. You can waste your time. You can sit in circles, absorb all kinds of psychological influences, exhaust your own, and in many cases become so filled up with contending influences that you are in a state of psychological fever all the time, and so exhaust yourself that you will become as limp and useless as a rag.

This is not the way to use the opportunities you have, and you should avoid the insane methods of development of many who are extremely anxious to develop you as mediums.

It may be thought that we are speaking against our own cause. It may occur to you that the greater the number of mediums, the greater the army that is dispensing truth throughout the world. Let us caution you that the development of mediumship ought not to be the highest aim of individual existence.

There are duties to be done here, soil to be cultivated, people to be clothed, honourable service to be given to humanity at large. It is but fair and just return for all the privileges and advantages conferred upon you, to build up the constitution of human society wisely and truly. These things will infinitely bless and better the world, and give you a nobler purpose in life than will the development of mediumship which, in some cases, has no other result than a gratifying of vanity or a craving after notoriety.

Sensible Growth

Mediumship, when it comes spontaneously and manifests itself unsought and uncalled-for, is the type of mediumship which is likely to be the most satisfactory. Sensibly developed and carefully prosecuted, it establishes mental harmony, order, peace and stability. On the other hand, when the vital powers are depleted, mediumship does develop a class of poor, hollow-voiced and pale-faced creatures that the world calls mediums. Much depends on the means that are used.

The true cultivation of mediumship is a stepping stone to the exercise of your own spiritual powers. Where the individual is always the subject of a dominant and controlling power, no real advantage to the individual accrues. But when you can go progressively forward and reach that spiritual consciousness of the existence of the powers belonging to your own spirit, you open a door to introduce yourself into the spiritual state. You can express through the outer life what you gather therein.

Mediumship leads on to a personal, practical knowledge of how to utilize your interior latent spiritual powers. You may be inspired, and by that inspiration your mind will be illuminated and your soul expanded. Sensibly developed, you will be rounded and strengthened in character and nature, and you can become a healer, a helper, a teacher of the world aided by the powers of the immortal life that shall work within you.

And as you rightly use mediumship and reverently pursue it, and labour for its highest and best advantage, it will inform you of your spiritual possibilities here and now. But better than all, it will enable you to crown your days with health of body, soundness of mind and purity of soul. When accompanied with these three divine possessions, life becomes a long dream of use and beauty to your fellows and to yourselves.

These are the results that shall crown your efforts as you march up through the pathways of mediumship, into the better and far more delightful ways of true spiritual growth and unfoldment.

Heart of the Matter

A spiritual religion is not an institutional matter. It is not a question of ritual, creed, sacraments or sacrifices. It is better than all such matters. In this life, it is the outflow of the inmost principles of Love, Truth and Wisdom and their practical application to the business of daily life. It is the living today, so that the soul remains unclouded by fears regarding tomorrow, whether that tomorrow refers to this world or the next. It is the realization that God, Nature and Humanity are one glorious and wondrous whole. Based upon these points, religious teaching would be broad, humane and tolerant.

Some people look upon mediumistic phenomena as quite detached from any religious value or ethical importance. But is not this an incompatible position to occupy? For, admitting that the phenomena are produced by men and women who have survived death, there cannot be more conclusive evidences showing that we survive death. The basis of spiritual religion is knowledge of one's nature, here and hereafter. Survival of death is as natural as survival of sleep.

Our religious teaching must run hand in hand with our knowledge of the future life and its realities, else what further follies than those that have already cursed the world may be taught regarding the hereafter – high heaven only knows!

In the words of William Stainton Moses, "There is an intelligent operator at the other end of the line." The objective facts of the spiritual life have always been the foundation of religion. But fear, credulity and ignorance have led to bigotry and superstition in the past. Religion has been sought outside the human being, so it became material and debased.

The proper understanding of the lessons to be drawn from mediumistic phenomena lead to the foundations of a truly spiritual religion, a religion that shall meet the needs of the head and heart, and assist in ushering in that blessed era when the unity of humankind and the federation of the world shall be an accomplished fact.

Special Gifts

We have no sort of sympathy with the doctrine that makes mediumship a gift from God to a mortal. God never gives special gifts to anyone. There are no favourites. Why should there be? God regulates and orders existence in every department in divine equality; and, latently, every individual possesses precisely the same qualities. True, it appears that the exercise of mediumship today is special and particular, but it is the manifestation of a universal possibility which will ultimately be realized by all humankind.

We want it distinctly understood that all the stories you have read of mediumship being a special gift from God, and of the angels coming down and giving you this gift or the other gift, or that you must be the seventh daughter of a seventh daughter, and all such kind of nonsense, are absolutely absurd. No mortal or spirit can put into a human being what is not there now. What can be done is this: the hidden spring may be touched so that, that which has not been hitherto known to exist, may be developed and brought into exercise. But this is a very different thing from giving you a gift or putting something into your nature that did not previously exist therein.

Many people consider that mediumship is the greatest possible blessing that can come to them, while others would not have it under any circumstances, considering it to be dangerous to health and morals. When asked to consider whether mediumship is a thing to be sought for and an experience that is calculated to benefit all individuals, our judgement is clear and decided: it is not a thing to be sought for and it cannot always be considered a blessing to the person who experiences it.

It must always be borne in mind that those characteristics of your life's expression that are spontaneously made manifest, are the best for you in their expression and in their results. Those faculties that have to be forced into activity, and require constant nursing and care to maintain in operation, will entail such drains upon body, mind and spirit that the benefits to you in the end are highly questionable.

When mediumship expresses itself spontaneously, manifesting itself by reason of its own inherent power, there can be no question that, rightly used and with proper rational limits, the exercise of mediumship can be made a means of great blessing to the individual and the community as well. However, the persistent effort to force it into activity should always be discouraged.

There are so many other things so far as the practical necessities of human life are concerned. It is better to attend to the pressing needs of this world's life, education and development than to squander precious powers and energies in order to develop a flower that, perchance, may bloom for a season and then wither and die, leaving scarcely a memory of its hue and fragrance behind.

The Divinity Within: A Trance Address

When the world grows wise enough, and clearly sees the character of God's great government, it will universally concede that the gifts of God are good eternally. It is not in trampling beneath your feet the talents bestowed by God that you are going to attain real progress; but in applying them intelligently and wisely to the purpose and desires of your life. For your nature needs its true unfoldment in order that latent qualities and powers may be brought to the surface and stimulated.

We have so profound a faith in, and so deep a worship for the divinity of mankind, that at times we feel that if the world's humanity were only what that humanity can become, the world would need no service from the spirit world to aid it in its upward progress.

There is so much of good, so much of truth, so much of power and beauty enshrined within this nature of yours. We feel and know how divinely great this humanity can be. "Over there" then, where love is the ruling element, the individual unfolds every latent element of the divine humanity, and realizes fully and completely all the elements of human greatness.

Die to the old and live to the new; die to the false and live to the true. And by so dying and so coming to life you can attain a freedom and an impetus of development that cannot come to you by any other means. There are hatreds that will have to die before love can bloom; there is ignorance that must die ere wisdom can take its place; there is the calloused cold-heartedness that must die ere the warm rich life of love can animate the soul itself. There are all these influences to die from, ere the jewels of character and the beauties of the inner life can fill your mind.

J.M. Peebles

J.M. Peebles
1822-1922
American Minister, Physician
Author, Peace Activist

Debra Skelton

J.M. Peebles

Refreshing Preaching

My Tradition

At Funerals

Refreshing Preaching

The clergy announce the subject of their addresses these days as a sort of stool pigeon enticement to draw in the fluttering, floating crowd. The *Sunday Morning Chronicle* – a paper, by the way, that refuses to publish notices of Spiritualist meetings under "Religious Meetings" – contained the following notice under the heading of *Religious Intelligence:*

> "The subject of discourse at Dr. Gray's church tonight will be: The incidents of the flood; the Ark; the builder of the Ark; description of the Ark itself; its stormy passage and the place where it anchored."

Important religious intelligence – *truly?* With all due deference, we seriously inquire what the people of this country care about Noah's Ark. Is it not more legitimate to deal with loss of life and causes of the same? No matter how the Israelites were fed, are the poor of this country in each city, hamlet and neighbourhood all fed? We must deal with the living present, the necessities of this age.

Oh, for men and women to occupy the pulpits speaking words that convince, words that touch the heart's deepest affections, words that move people to that broad humanitarian plane of toleration and justice!

My Tradition

Spirit is God. Spiritualism does not rest entirely upon phenomena but on spirit. Spirit is the substantial reality. And you are a spirit now, a spirit living in a material body. The human being is a trinity in unity, constituted of a body, a soul and a conscious undying spirit – the divine Ego. Spirits are but men and women divested of their mortal bodies. They walk by our side often, and yet unseen. Spirit permeates and energizes the matter of all kingdoms: mineral, vegetable and animal.

There is but one world and that world embraces the yesterdays, the todays and the innumerable tomorrows of eternity.

Columbus concluded that if there was a "this side" there must necessarily be a "that side" to the world. And likewise this world indicates another, a future world which the Spiritualists have fully described. Spiritualism does not create truth, but is witness to the truth of a future existence.

There have been visions, trances, apparitions and conscious spirit communications all through the past ages. They happened in the past and they occur today. Spiritualism unlocks the mysteries of the ages, which constitute the foundation stones of all the ancient faiths and gave to the world its inspired teachers and immortal leaders. The essence of Spiritualism is found in the inspired teachings of all sacred books.

Spiritualist practice without the Spirit, without religion or moral growth, is but the veriest rust and rubbish. And religion, by whatever name it is known, without its accompanying spiritual gifts is only an empty shell. Everyone can cultivate that loving kindness which disarms resentment, that patience which endures suffering, that gentleness which neutralizes acidity of temper, that forgiveness which obliterates personal animosities, that consciousness of right which inspires justice, and that tender charity which makes the harmonial being. Those who war against God and immortality war against the Divine Spirit. Spiritualism not only demonstrates future existence, but it encourages invention, art, science and exploration, and strikes the chains from millions of slaves.

When Spiritualism in its divinest aspects is literally practised, our country will be the universe, our home the world, our rest wherever human hearts beat in sympathy with our own, and the highest happiness of each will be altruism. This is Spiritualism, pure, simple and practical.

At Funerals

When the mortal sleeps the sleep of death, and the soul is marching on, the eyes of the loving left behind are tearful, and their hearts heave and ache. The one who is passing may be a father or mother, sister or brother, who in life professed and prized the principles of Spiritualism.

The day of burial comes and who ministers at the altar of consolation? A Spiritualist teacher? A seer with vision open to the glories of the eternal? Oh no! A sectarian clergyman is invited, one who knows little of the nature of death, of the condition of the departed, or of the activities that make radiant the spiritual world.

Is this showing a proper respect to the ascended soul of the loved one? Is it honouring the truth? Is it honouring our principles? And unless we honour them, how can we expect others to?

Those Spiritualists dedicated to voicing the truths of the Harmonial Philosophy are particularly fitted to minister words of comfort at funerals and words of beauty at the marriage altar. If Spiritualists desire to claim the respect of a thinking community, they must first respect themselves, respect their principles, and practise them in spirit and in letter.

Debra Skelton

Emma Hardinge Britten

Emma Hardinge Britten
1823-1899
British Medium, Author, Activist
Artist, Inspirational Speaker
Founding Editor: *The Two Worlds*
Coalesced the *Principles of Modern Spiritualism*

Debra Skelton

Emma Hardinge Britten

I Am Introduced

A few days ago I received a letter from the esteemed editor of *Two Worlds*, Mr. E.W. Wallis, asking me to contribute to the columns of his paper upon "Spiritualism: Past, Present and Future," on the occasion of the fiftieth year since the movement known as Modern Spiritualism was revealed to humanity.

The now world-wide movement has grown out of the humblest and least remarkable of beginnings. It has worked its way from the influence of two children from an almost unknown village in America, until it has shaken the whole world, and that in the face of the bitterest opposition. In only fifty years, it has captured the public acceptance of kings, princes, nobles and thousands of literary and scientific supporters. I will condense my own early experiences into a brief narration of my conversion to the great modern movement.

It must be nearly forty years since I went for the first time in my life to America to fill an engagement at the Broadway Theatre in New York. Boarding accommodation had been secured for me and my mother, who always accompanied me. I had only been a few days in my new quarters when I became astonished and shocked to hear many of the boarders coolly talking about the "spirits" of those the world called dead. My new acquaintances spoke as if they were all alive again and in constant communication with their earthly friends.

At the boarding table these people made frequent arrangements when and where to meet to commune with "ghosts" and at last shocked me so greatly that I could bear it no longer. When next I met with the gentleman who had arranged my board in that dreadful house, I poured out my complaints to him and declared my intention not to remain in that ill-omened place any longer. My amazement may be understood when I found that the gentlemen to whom I made my complaints not only laughed at my scruples, but owned that he himself was a firm believer in what the world (at least in America) called Spiritualism. He added that I should find all the theatrical company of which I was a member of the same belief.

Finding at last that escape from this spiritualistic society was at present hopeless, I made up my mind as quietly as possible to avoid all discussion on the odious subject, to fill out my allotted time in my engagement, and when that was ended, to return with my good mother to our own country and never again set foot in that ghostly, heretical America.

Determining, however, to find out what these dreadful Spiritualists did or believed, so that when I returned to England I could expose them and warn others against their impious tricks, I finally consented to accompany my friend, Mr. Fenno, to what he termed a spiritual medium's séance. Mr. Fenno did not introduce me by name, but simply said I was a lady who wished for a spirit sitting. I sat in morose silence until I was startled by loud knockings just under the hand I had carelessly laid on the table. "There they are," said my hostess without moving from her seat in the window.

Determined to find out who and what the "they" were, I hastily drew off the tablecloth and then turned the table over in order to find the springs which I felt sure must have been the source of the sounds produced. While I was engaged carefully looking for the springs, no sign of which could I discover, I heard loud knockings on the floor beneath my very feet.

Determined to sift this horrid fraud (as I deemed it then) to its very source, I was down on the ground instantly, feeling the floor. Whilst still vainly searching for the locomotive springs, there came a knocking with even greater force than ever on the wall opposite me. Feeling suddenly and strangely overcome by these mysterious sounds, I sank back again into my chair, my dear little hostess evidently pitying my bewilderment.

For the two hours I remained in that room I found, by the telegraphic signals of the invisible rappers, that I had never lost a friend or even an acquaintance who did not come back. It proved to me, beyond a shadow of doubt, that there was no death.

Since this, my initial lesson, I became a medium myself and sat for the public of New York and other cities until my duties as a lecturer compelled me to the world-wide travels which the spirits mapped out for me. All over the forty-six states of America, Canada, India, Australia, New Zealand, nearly all the countries of Europe, often in the palaces of princes, and among many of the profoundest scientists of this my native land, I have been received and welcomed by many devoted Spiritualists, like my dear friends the Fox Family, D.D. Home, Andrew Jackson Davis and hundreds of others. But the end is not yet, or even in prospect....

For the present, I close my paper given in honour of, and with humble reverence for, the first fifty years of Modern Spiritualism, with the following words spoken by my dear old friend, Victor Hugo:

> "There is no more death; that which is called so only liberates the soul from its mortal envelope. From the humblest worm to the mightiest man, we take the next step beyond earth, upward and onward for ever through all eternity."

Nature of Your Spirit

Tonight, it is our purpose to consider that magnificent element which vitalizes your own existence – the spirit within you. Up to this age, the world's opinions upon this point have been opinions merely.

Knowledge is power. The knowledge which you possess of yourselves will open a vast vista concerning your own destiny. The principles of Spiritualism, rather than the phenomena, are now demanded. What is spirit? Whence its origin? What is its destiny?

We remark that a human has a structure: a body, a life and a spirit. The body is matter; life, that electricity which we claim to be the tool that acts upon matter; and spirit, the guiding principle that controls and directs it.

We find that there are times when the spirit acts independently of that which you term life, in the condition called sleep. In visions of the night, your spirit is active. Your consciousness is taking cognizance of scenes far remote from where your body is still in existence. In sleep, that life is beating and visible in every pulse and through every vein; and yet the spirit is absolutely separated from it, just as the consciousness of distant scenes is removed from the place where your body lies. Similarly, in the state termed clairvoyance, there is no action of will. The spirit is far away and yet the life is present and so is the body. In that other condition, that of the corpse, the uses of the body are ended and the warm quivering life has now left forever; yet the spirit continues. We could instance innumerable other illustrations to prove to you that the body is the tenement of the spirit; but life itself is not the thought, is not the spirit.

There is something so powerful, so tremendous in the awful view of the inert form from which the spirit has passed, that man has marked terror upon it because he is in ignorance of what change means. We acknowledge that it is the absence of the spirit. The spirit, then, was the organism, the spirit was the power, the spirit was the spring, the reason and the guide.

We have heard the materialist declare that humans were but machines which only subsisted so long as you placed the fire, the wood, the stone, the water and the wheels in proximity, one with another. Destroy the machine, says the materialist, and you destroy the power. Oh materialist, how little you know!

The machine is but the expression of the power, the outward effect of the power. The power is indestructible. The fire will blaze and the heat will circle around you, for you cannot put it out of existence though you break up ten thousand machines. The elements of being are there forever.

The form is only the vehicle for their expression. The real power is within.

Mourning

Is there any one of you that has not seen the fading form of father, mother, companion or child pass from your side into the unrelenting grasp of death? Have you watched these beloved ones, day by day, grow weaker and fainter, the eye's lustre fade, the waxen impress of inevitable decay steal over the pale white cheek and faded brow?

Physicians' skill, love, wealth – all fail then. Nothing can keep back the parting soul from the great mystery of the unknown hand, which seems to be tugging at the silver cords of life with the mighty power that mortal hand would vainly strive to restrain. When the last dread hour of parting came at length, and you laid your dead away and felt that a star was gone out from heaven; and that once familiar voice was no longer; and the streets were cold and the house was empty; and something was missing that changed the whole tone and current of your life – what would you have given if you could then have been told that the dead one was by your side?

Widow, if you could have known that your companion still was there, and that there was a power guarding you stronger even than the arm of flesh. Country, that hast mourned thy patriots, couldst thou have known that in another land they still laboured for earth. Fathers, mothers, friends, would you not have hailed such a mighty revelation, the soul's eternal triumph over the grave? Death, like pain, we blindly call the enemy until, on the day of spiritual revelation, we discover that it opens the door for the soul to immortal life and freedom, when the teachings of earthly pain are forever ended and their mission done.

What It Is and What It Is Not

Spiritualism is not a religion – it is religion per se. It has no fixed creed and is not binding upon any human soul that is not convinced of its truth by sufficient evidence. It may be in harmony with many religions, writings or laws of science but is independent of all these, emerging by virtue of spiritual laws, absolute and true, whether man understands them or not.

Spiritualism applies in general to the communion of spiritual beings with mortals. It does not originate in any human theories or opinions. Its communications proceed wholly from those who are *in* the actual experience. It derives no authority from books written by mankind, whether ancient or modern, whether labeled sacred or profane.

The term "modern spiritualism" signifies the discovery of a mode whereby the spirits can communicate systematically with earth. The communicants are the spirits of men, women and children who once lived on earth and are now in the continuity of life, personal identity and all that made them individuals. These communicants are in varied states of growth and all are stimulated onwards to progress. No bad spirit can compel a mortal to do wrong any more than a bad human companion can do so. The wrong doer is himself the real actor. It is only a subterfuge to allege that evil spirits can influence man to do wrong.

The ancient seer, prophet or magian and the modern medium are one and the same in organic nature, possessed of his or her faculties only as the result of certain physiological and natural qualities and not by virtue of any special morality, goodness or the favour of the Creator. All human beings are spirits, and the body is only an external mould in which spirit becomes individualized. All powers exercised by spirits pertain as much to the human spirit now as ever they will do in the hereafter. If all mortals cannot exercise these powers, it is only on account of the lack of knowledge concerning spiritual things in which the world has been kept.

It is just as natural to communicate with each other when one party is on earth and the other in the spirit world, as it was when both parties were on earth. Spirits are drawn by affection to commune with those they have left behind. Such a communion establishes the existence and nature of spirit and, inferentially, of God the Spirit.

Every living being is susceptible to spiritual impressions; whether mortals know it or not, spirits associate as a soul world to this natural world. Therefore, the knowledge of their existence, their communion with earth, the demonstrations they bring of immortality and the existence of God the Spirit, constitute the essence of true religion.

Footprints of the Pioneers

Time is the great and original touchstone of truth.

When the great spiritual outpouring of the nineteenth century shall be submitted to the judgment of posterity; and the criterion of time, unbiased by passion or prejudice, shall determine its true value to mankind, the more eagerly will humanity search for the footprints of its pioneers.

Will Spiritualism be absorbed by sectarian organizations and used simply as an agent for the promotion of liberal ideas? Or will it remain a concrete movement, itself absorbing other religious associations in the vortex of its irrepressible powers of demonstration and reason? Will the spirits continue to experiment until they have perfected their glorious telegraph between heaven and earth? Or, weary of our apathy and shortcomings, will they permit glimpses only of the possibilities that lie dormant within the human soul and then leave the earth to await the uprising of a more faithful and spiritually-minded generation?

These are questions upon which we have formed widely diverse opinions and the results shall be proven in time. But the immense importance of clear, concise histories of what has been done, said, thought and suffered in the earlier phases of this movement can never be exaggerated. The records of all this should be preserved as milestones on the road of human progress, without which the pilgrims of the future are liable to fall into precisely the same snares as have beset the paths of the pioneers.

Debra Skelton

Seven Sabbaths

Spiritualism belongs to no age, no country and no special class of mind. It is the acknowledgement of the spiritual origin of all things and the unfoldment of those mystic ties that bind the soul to its Author. It discloses to us the nature, quality, possible destiny and absolute relation of the human soul to immortality.

If Spiritualism were nothing more than the enjoyment of the hour, beautiful as it is, gladdening to the heart and cheering to the mourner, we would have no need to herald it forth to the world. But Spiritualism teaches of that God who is Spirit, of that immortality which constitutes the very gist of human existence, of that life-practice for which it has been established as a guide. What more do we require to constitute the elements of a religion? If it is not a religion, it is nothing.

Spiritualism is a living, vital religion. Religion with Spiritualists is not a mere Sabbath-day affair. Religion with them seeks seven Sabbaths instead of one, demands that every place shall be a church as well as the house that mankind has consecrated. Spiritualism requires that every deed shall be an act of prayer and every thought a form of worship.

Gordon Higginson

Gordon Higginson
1918-1993
British Healer, Medium, Teacher

Debra Skelton

Gordon Higginson

Not Just for the Few

Embracing the Foe

Listening

Not Just For the Few

I often regret the passing of the old-style lyceums. I was a member of the lyceum from a very early age. I was not taught just about spirit but about my own self.

I found confidence in doing things for other people. I learned all about service to my fellow human being. I am glad that there seems to be a revival in the lyceum movement for the young. In my day, there were so many; nearly every church had its own lyceum. We were taught that we had a responsibility, here and now, to make sure that this life had meaning. In these groups, we learned we could not always like each other, but because of the spirit which unites us, we must endeavour to love each person we meet. That has been a tremendous help to me in my life, when I have had to face such difficult and sad experiences with other people.

The young are our future. If we do not take the time to train them in the ways of the Spirit, we are neglecting our own future. After all the suffering and bloodshed of the Great Wars and despite the advanced knowledge of today, the world sometimes seems to be no better or more sane. We make the same mistakes again and again, create the same conditions of hunger and want throughout the world, continually neglecting our true nature to pursue a dream of avarice and power.

This must change. The responsibility for that change is ours. We cannot delay. We cannot leave this until tomorrow. We owe this effort to our children and to their children.

Spiritualism is a sane and rational religion. I truly believe it is the hope for humanity's future. I also believe it is the only religion which has taken change into its basic understanding.

People seek to achieve a more spiritual way of life. Many are turning to religious philosophies which give a feeling of security by promising that, if the individual fulfills a strict program, they will be rewarded. They hope that, by being more severe and austere in their religious practices, they can atone. But earthly practices and a God of wrath will not change the heart of a person.

As Spiritualists, our concern must be with the world situation. Mankind has become so dangerous to itself that the nations of the world have no alternative but to learn to embrace our principle of unity if they want to avoid destruction. Spiritualism's future is not to be kept just for the few, but for the whole of humanity. We must let people see the wonderful things we've experienced; not to convince, but to prove why we are committed to this way.

Embracing the Foe

I do not think we are of any use to the spirit world as mediums, leaders or people to respect if we expect everything to go easily for us. We do make foes. One of the things Silver Birch taught me was that, if you do not make an enemy, then your work has not been of use to mankind. The great guide said this to me in an hour of sorrow. I took such comfort from these words. They seemed to give a dimension to my difficulties which I had not been able to perceive. I had to stop and think more about my troubles, but in a very different way.

Remember, all that lies ahead is there. We are sowing seeds today that will bring about vast changes in the world of tomorrow. On one of my visits to the Silver Birch circle, I asked about the future of Spiritualism. Silver Birch told me that the Great Spirit knows what's going on. The Great Spirit will bring in, at the right time, those who will do the work and be able to help humanity. I have often thought of those words and that it was a long time in coming. But to my pleasant surprise, I now have those I love dearly among young people, those who I look upon as sons and daughters. They have some remarkable gifts.

So I have lost one of my fears about passing over, for I have wondered who will take on the yoke of responsibility which I have carried. I have been able to see for myself and help many young mediums so they do not encounter the pitfalls I did. They will go further ahead and add to my mediumship, for they see it in a different way than I saw it in the past.

There is an awakening. I see a hunger for a new vision of life. The door to a spiritual vista will open when we allow the flow of inner impressions to break into our souls and guide our lives. When we bring the love of God, and the deep inner desire to serve only God into our lives, then we will understand our relationship with all life. In this state of awareness there is inspiration from those in the spirit life; we must not fail them.

Listening

When you pray, you become the prayer. We understand that God is an inner power, not an outside one. When you ask for something in prayer, it is no use expecting an outside power to come along and give you what you have requested. But if you can become your prayer through the sincerity and depth of your thoughts, then you have the answer.

Each person will experience prayer in their own way because each of us is different. There are some who will use a formula, but I do not think that this has great value. When you use the same words over and over, they become at best not a prayer but a mantra, and that is a different matter entirely. Prayer must be stimulated from the heart, not the memory.

Prayer is not all about asking, even when we think that we are asking for the right things. Prayer is listening, communicating, being at one with reality; the reality of God. In prayer, we become our God. And if we listen we are given the answers, the strength and knowledge to see through our troubles, not from an outside source but from our inner reality.

In that touching of our soul with the Great Soul of the Universe, we are filled with love and humility. We no longer want only for ourselves,

Debra Skelton

but also for that which is right for humanity. It may be that we have our part to play. Then we will be given the strength of purpose to fulfill our task. It might be that we have to stand back and allow events to shape our lives, so we are given the understanding which helps us to do this.

It can take many years to learn to pray properly. Some will never learn. But all the time we have to try. Of course, the more we try, the better we get.

I have sometimes been filled with the most complete feeling of love and belonging through prayer. Then I know I am in touch. When I thank God for all that I have, I am reminded of that which has been given to me. When I give thanks, I am reminded forcibly of the beauty of the universe and I am with God.

I always think that part of our prayers should be an acknowledgement of the closeness of the spirit world, not because my friends in that world need to be reminded; but because I, a human soul, need to be reminded of that love which is given so freely from those realms.

Prayer crystallizes within you what you are feeling about yourself, about your fellow man and about your God. It is an expression of where you are and what you are. If you have absorbed the love of God and Spirit, this will be manifest in your prayer. If you have a sincere desire to help and to make progress, this will be heard.

We have all that is needed within us.

Maurice Barbanell

Maurice Barbanell
1902-1981
British Medium, Journalist, Lecturer
Founding Editor: *Psychic News*

Debra Skelton

Maurice Barbanell

Spiritual United Nations

Modern Revelation

Miracles

Spiritual United Nations

One day after death you will be precisely the same individual as you were the day before, except that you will have discarded your physical body. Death comes when the real you withdraws itself and functions through your spirit body.

Life in the spirit world is not hazy, unsubstantial or nebulous. It is both foolish and erroneous to imagine that, when we pass from this life, we sleep forever or until such time as there will be a resurrection. Death is resurrection.

When we die, there is no great judge on a white throne separating the sheep from the goats; for we have judged ourselves in the spiritual nature we have attained by the character we have formed. That is our spiritual passport.

Human relationships will be altered by the appreciation of spiritual life. Differences of colour, creed, race, language and nationality will be superseded by the prevailing knowledge of one's spiritual nature. In essence, the same spirit is within every human being in the world. You do not have to die to become a spiritual being; you are a spiritual being today.

The simple truth is that God has made us all of one spirit. The universal laws have so ordained it. Members of every race, irrespective of the colour of their skins, are spiritual kith and kin. Spiritually we are all children in the divine family. This is, in fact, the spiritual United Nations.

Modern Revelation

I see in Spiritualism part of a great plan to unify all religions and all peoples. Its evidence is that there are no Jewish, Protestant, Roman Catholic, Baptist or Hindu souls. When the scales drop from our eyes, we begin to realize that spiritually we belong to no nation, race or religion.

Spirit, being the common denominator, unites people. Theology, with its belief in monopoly or special dispensation, creates barriers of strife and even hatred. How can theology, which emanates from the mind, compare with inspiration which emanates from divine sources?

Spiritualism, when fully understood, is unconcerned with any brand of theology. It is concerned with the demonstration of spiritual facts which compel us to realize our relationship with every other individual and with the power which endowed us with life. Evidence of spiritual realities as the foundation will enrich humanity and provide conditions in which the whole person, not only the body, obtains the fullest expression.

Spiritualism shows that there is nothing to fear in death or in life. The light of spirit truth is there to guide us how to live, so that when we pass we are filled with no regrets because we will know that our earthly pilgrimage was not in vain.

This is the modern revelation. This is the truth which every reasonable human being can prove for themselves.

Miracles

The power of the spirit has always been at work, adapting itself through the centuries to the needs, understanding and capacity of its recipients. The Bible, like many other sacred books, is a testament to spirit activity. Whether many of its characters are called prophets, seers or mediums makes no difference. They were all the instruments of higher power which, as it flowed through human channels, produced signs and wonders which were mistakenly regarded as miracles.

Each revelation was tempered to the age and country in which it appeared. The new revelation usually came through a great medium who first attracted public attention by the psychic phenomena that occurred in that person's presence. They would then drive home the ethical principles which became the foundation of all world religions.

Whatever happened in the past, in any part of the world, was due to the operation of natural laws. To alter or suspend them implies a criticism of the governing intelligence, which has to intervene because events are temporarily out of control; and that would mean that the Deity is neither omniscient nor omnipotent.

The laws of God are the same yesterday, today and forever. There can be no divine love for the year arbitrarily called one, that is not equally available for any year in the twentieth century.

Hudson and Emma Rood Tuttle

Hudson Tuttle
1836-1910
and
Emma Rood Tuttle
1837-1916
American Authors, Educators, Activists

Debra Skelton

Hudson and Emma Rood Tuttle

A Change of Sphere

Compassion

World Citizens

A Change of Sphere

Death is not a change of being. It is a change of sphere. The Spirit, whether in the body or out of it, is the same. The one who goes out of the door of his house is the same individual that he was within.

We must regard matter and spirit as equally sacred. As long as we are inhabitants of this sphere, our physical being is essential, and the laws and conditions of its development are as holy as that of the spirit.

We have an exalted Nature, capable of infinite possibilities. When the physical side shall melt, and the world on which it depends passes away, that Nature will only have begun its unfolding.

In the tangled web of mortal life, we still inquire, as did the sages of old, what is truth? What is right? What wrong? Most perfectly does Spiritualism answer. She has no word of condemnation for the wrong-doer, but for the wrong. She utters no word of praise for those who never stumble. She makes no distinction in the breadth of her benevolence. Her voice is melodious with love while it speaks of eternal justice.

Listen to her voice and learn how it is possible to triumph over the accidents of mortal life, meeting all its duties and bearing all its burdens with cheerful heart, laying the deep foundations of that temple immortal, beyond the shadow of death....

Compassion

Everyone moves in their limited sphere. Everyone has their inheritance of accumulated ancestral wrongs, misdeeds and errors. Everyone has their motives, reasons and causes for their actions, known only to themselves, which none other can know. We think, not knowing these causes that, were we thus placed, we should do differently. A moment's reflection will assure us we would do exactly the same.

Debra Skelton

Inasmuch as we help others, we grow strong. When we bend to give a helping hand to the fallen we are ennobled. One attribute goes forth always to return, bearing rich reward, and that is love. It is yielding as thinnest air, yet firm. It is as gentle as the breath of the south wind, yet the strongest force in the universe. It looks backward as well as forward. It reaches down to draw those below up to its vantage ground and reaches upward in its aspirations, giving all without expectancy of return. This is the power which shall redeem the world.

One of the most ancient of Chinese sages, Lautsze, said, "The sage does not lay up treasures. The more he does for others the more he has of his own. The more he gives to others, the more he is increased." These are words of wisdom. The more the sage teaches, the more perfectly he understands his own doctrine; and his own torch is not dimmed, though it light ten thousand others.

World Citizens

Let us benefit the children to be born a hundred years hence by educating aright the children of today.

The child is the base of the individual, and individuals combined give us world conditions. Individuals may give us world betterment or produce world deterioration. Education should promote growth, physically, intellectually and morally; steady growth from the kindergarten on through the university. We want physical growth and instructors who will not do anything to interfere with it. They may unwittingly do many things which interfere with the laws of health and thus prevent the best physical development. Some teachers starve the students for fresh, pure air; some keep them in as a punishment or detain them after school. These things may seriously affect health and the ability to learn. The mind cannot act clearly when the body is uncomfortable.

Intellectual education is the one thing never overlooked in our schools. Too often we see bright minds but weak bodies. We want goodness as well as brightness. It is just as useful and should be cultivated constantly. Our teachers should be required to be versed in this part of education. Unfortunately, it is not in our curriculum.

We must admit that a knowledge of the right methods of juvenile culture is a knowledge second to none in importance. These topics should occupy the highest place in the course of instruction passed through by each man and woman, especially those who expect to be professional educators.

Care is taken to fit youth for society, but no care whatever to fit them for the still more responsible position of parents. It seems to be the prevailing idea that, for this, no preparation is needed. They are supposed to be born with all that wisdom in them, which is a great mistake. Three lines of education – physical, intellectual and moral – should be worked together through all the years devoted to learning to live, which is the true aim of study. The requisite qualification for this should be furnished in our schools. How much it is needed is made plain by the great number of divorces and unjustly treated children. The genuine character-building which will fit them for half-partnership in a home where they can be trusted, and be prime factors in the welfare of the nation, is as yet only an ideal in the minds of those who see the need of better methods.

Andrew Jackson Davis

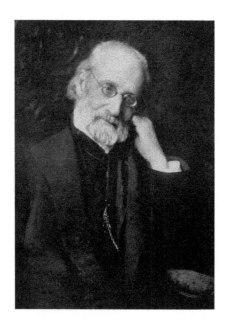

Andrew Jackson Davis
1826-1910
American Visionary
Author, Humanitarian
Father of Modern Spiritualism

Debra Skelton

Andrew Jackson Davis

Truth

A Truthful Mind

Truth

There is a simplicity, a beauty, a majesty, belonging to the Principle of Truth. But what is truth?

According to my impressions, the truth is something more than that which endures only for a time. Anything which is temporary, fleeting and evanescent as the passing breeze should not be dignified with the name of, nor receive the esteem which belongs properly to, truth. Truth is the same yesterday, today and forever. It is the same always and everywhere.

When Isaac Newton saw the apple fall to the earth, he did not regard that circumstance as an eternal truth, but simply an illustration of some great natural principle. And when he probed the secrets of creation and discovered what he termed the Law of Gravitation, he drew a line of distinction between the falling of that single apple and the principle whereby all apples fall.

Newton did not invent the Law of Gravitation, nor did he find it; for it was never lost. It was then, always had been, and will always continue to be, the universal revelation of the spirit of God.

The Bible is supposed, by many, to be God's eternal word; but most believers fail to discriminate between the book itself and the truths which it contains. And others again confuse the writers with the truths they wrote, thus making the divinity of the ten commandments to rest on Moses, and the doctrine of immortality to rest on Jesus. If a doctrine is eternally true, it depends no more upon the existence of Moses or Jesus, than the Law of Gravitation depends upon the existence of Isaac Newton.

God's truth is absolute.

Now, I ask, which deserves to be termed truth – the falling of the apple, or that immutable and magnificent Principle by which the universe rolls through the realms of Infinitude? Methinks you answer – the Principle is the Truth!

A Truthful Mind

The highest and richest inheritance is a truthful mind, a mind so honest with itself that it can give true utterance to whatever is found hidden within the soul. Such a mind perceives and delights in reporting things as they are. It is not a mechanical, stilted, frigid mind; its thoughtfulness and natural logic are flowings of Intuition's fountains.

Intuition is the inwrought wisdom of the Eternal Spirit. Acquired information is the kit of tools by which the intuitive or inspired mind demonstrates its truths, its hidden melody. Sincerity and candour are effects, of which integral love and the daily practice of truth are the causes. Inherent love of truth is an immortal love which transforms the soul into the image and likeness of the gods.

This standard being uplifted, the world is discovered to be teeming with unbalanced, unhappy and therefore untruthful characters. Here is a person with large intellectual abilities, but heartless and false in relation to his fellow being. There is another, filled with the most tender sympathies, ever ready to do a friendly deed, but deficient in the wisdom principle.

Likewise, in the religious world, we observe two extremely oppositional classes: those of sentiment without principle and those of principle without sentiment. To gratify the devout aspirations of the Christian sentimentalist, graceful ceremonies magnetize the reasoning faculties into a dreamy slumber. Though it temporarily pleases the half-awakened conscience, it indefinitely postpones the development of virtue and principle. We deplore a religious sentimentalist – a great heart with a small head minus the wisdom principle.

But the stilted rigidness and formalism of the unimaginative in religion are vices equally prejudicial to truthful progress. An unpoetical mind minus the spiritual sentiment is like a rich soil without flowers. Such a mind is at once uncharitable and untruthful.

Truth's clear-eyed genius ascends unfettered by selfishness or prejudice, with steps at once modest and deliberate. The truth-seeking mind goes forward with reservation and dignity. No white lies nestle and crawl within the spirit. They are always honest even when woefully mistaken. The truth lover is the best lover of humanity.

Will Ford

Will Ford
1913-unknown
British Minister, Medium, Healer
Father of Welsh Spiritualism

Debra Skelton

Will Ford

Spinners of Gold

Natural Philosophy

The Bigger Picture

Spinners of Gold

Think of Spirit in your meditation and work on the idea that it is the "beginning stuff" to the universe.

If that is the case, then think of your relationship with all other things: people, places, animals, ideas, everything. They are all connected. You are part of each other. Take as many years as you like to meditate on that. You will grow in your understanding of it. As you do so, put your understanding into action. This is not a plea to be trendy and environmental. It is a plea to be meaningfully, lovingly and respectfully part of the environment. Live out your understanding in practical terms.

Remember that you are free and spontaneous. You are not a set of mathematical calculations: you are never entirely predictable. This will give you a sense of freedom which is, in fact, the breath of life. You are not a robot. If anything, you are more like the passenger in the car. You are in charge of where you want to go. As you grow older, the car may not serve you quite as well, but it can never dictate to you entirely. You can always get out and walk when things get difficult!

Value spontaneity, and know you can never repeat any thing exactly. Each time life is a little different. For that reason (if you allow it to be) it is always interesting. For spirit to grow, it has to have free expression and needs an interested audience. Be spontaneous, be interested. That way you have provided a good environment for growth.

Learn the value of harmony. It is like sunshine to plants: without it there is no growth. Harmony is the result of love. It is a loving approach, a loving interpretation, a loving coming-together. Practise harmony in music, in colour, form, dance, in ideas, in friendship, in nature, in silence.

Dare to enjoy change and the unexpected. Remind yourself that change is life. That way you will train yourself out of the belief that growing old is growing "more dead" each day. What nonsense! All change is growth; all change is experience. You are becoming more you all the time.

Debra Skelton

You are a spinner of straw into gold. Work on the idea that, right now, you are in the place which is best for you. Whatever the joys or difficulties of now, they are gift-bearing moments for you. Ask yourself what it is they bring you, and learn from that. Every beauty is there for you to enjoy; every problem is a challenge for you to meet, beautifully. There is no moment which has no gift for you, no straw that will not become gold for you.

Natural Philosophy

The joy of gardening is the joy of watching changes unfold before your eyes. Where there is change there is life. Growth, the manifestation of life, is change.

Needless to say, all the natural world is teeming with life. We recognize that life, because things move, change their appearance, their sound, their smell and so on. My philosophy is one of change and growth. I call it natural philosophy because I am interested in excellence, not perfection; in life, not death. My philosophy has the label of Spiritualism, although that in itself may change because all living things do. For the moment, the word Spiritualism suits very well.

Spirit means life, and life is the most natural thing in the world. Mine is a natural philosophy. It is an approach to living which says that the changing life in a body is much more important than the body itself.

If you are like me, you will find the things you value most are not the physical ones. Materialism will not satisfy you. It will not satisfy you because you are alive and you change; material things do not live, do not change.

Furthermore, if you are looking for some ground rules on how best to live your life, a changeless philosophy, one that is totally abstract and unchanging, may not suit you; but natural philosophy might, simply because it grows with you and is a philosophy based on life and living.

Spiritualism is a religion which concentrates on the ever-living spirit of the individual. It does not say, "one day you will be perfect." Instead it teaches that, even beyond the death of your physical body, your spirit will continue to evolve eternally. It implies that even God is constantly evolving, for surely He, or She, or It, is also alive and therefore changing. You are not your body as materialists would suggest. You are merely in your body. The essential you is the life, the spirit within.

As a religion, Spiritualism is saying that the way to God is through tending your spirit. The first stage is to become aware of it. In a way it is saying that the most important things in a garden are the changes that happen in it, not the square yards of earth that it is made up of. What is important is how you use that earth to allow the changes of flower and fruit and growth to occur.

The Bigger Picture

To me the eternal theme of life is that life in every form is growing towards total consciousness – God consciousness. The pattern of all life can be traced in the growth, development and change that is all around you.

The grain of sand, the blade of grass, the moon above or the waters below – all things which exist are vital components of life's eternal pattern. Each pattern seems but some hint of a fuller pattern, and that pattern seems far from reach.

In a moment of questioning, we often feel that our hand is reaching out for light in a world of perpetual dark. In this mood, tense and still, there may come feelings which no word can explain; moments when we acknowledge that the very fact which allows us to question or wonder is, of itself, a miracle. Great and majestic are these moments when life seems neither right nor wrong, but simply inevitable.

Debra Skelton

The recognition of the scale of life is an early step in the individual's awareness of life's eternal theme. Certain laws at last become visible.

Animating life exists. Its habit is growth. Its growth is subject to law. Behind growth and its laws there is that which suggests a design. Somewhere within that which has been made visible there abides a pattern. That pattern is intention. Behind the intention there abides the Designer, the Grand Architect: God.

So life exists. It is characterized by growth. The growth is subject to law. The law is willed by God. We need to give up superstition, old patterns of thought which now prove to be false; we need to give up the idea that creation is the result of anything connected with chance or accident.

The governing laws and principles of life on its larger scale mimic the governing laws and principles on its smallest scale. What is true of the mass is true of each unit or cell. Each cell and each person, every moment of every day is subject to law. As Voltaire said, "Chance is a word void of sense; nothing can exist without a cause."

As far as I can understand it, that ultimate cause is the Will of God. Without that there is no law, no existence, no growth, no life. It is because all existence has one source, that there can be an eternal theme throughout all life.

Julia Schlesinger

Julia Schlesinger
1847-1929
American Author
Women's Rights Advocate
Editor: *The Carrier Dove, The Gleaner*

Debra Skelton

Julia Schlesinger

Work Enough for All

Believe in You

Humility

Discretion

Every Blade of Grass

Work Enough for All

No reformation can ever come except by persistent individual effort. Do not commence with your neighbours, but with yourselves. See to it that your own motives are unselfish. Never lose an opportunity of saying a kind word or reaching out a helping hand to any in despair, even though their own wrong-doing may have been the cause of their distress.

There is a higher and diviner life within reach of all, and within each person a spark of divinity which shall ultimately triumph over all untoward circumstances. Spiritualism has demonstrated the existence of the spiritual world of beauty lying all around you. It has made plain the way, which has been shrouded by theological inventions ready, apparently at every juncture, to pounce upon the unwary and hurl them into the pit of perdition.

Some people are inclined to dwell upon the glories of "over there" when the labours of this life are ended. They do not seem to realize that, here and now, the spirits who most need their care are those still dwelling in physical form; those in want of homes, food, clothing. Only so far as the teachings of any system can be made of practical use in the betterment of life are they of value to humanity.

Cultivate in yourself those attributes you have been accustomed to call divine. Be honest and true with one another. You may be able to deceive one another now, but there comes a time when you will stand in your true light, the masks will drop off, and you shall be known for just what you are, not what you seem to be. Then you will have to begin doing the things which should be done now. There is no royal road of ease, but work – earnest, helpful, noble work – for the good of all.

Meet together and discuss ways and means of usefulness. There is work enough for all, and you will be astonished at the results. Let a handful of devoted persons decide upon some special work, and enter into it with a divine purpose, and there is no possibility of failure. The good seeds may not at once germinate but, by and by, when the gentle rains of sorrow shall have watered them, and the sunshine of love revived

Debra Skelton

them, they will spring into beauteous life. Many capable, willing persons need only have the work mapped out for them and gladly they will enter into it. Harmonious cooperation is the only way of meeting the existing wrongs of society with any assurance of success.

Believe in You

Do not undertake anything until you are deeply imbued with its importance. Then bring into the work all the energies of soul of which you are possessed. If men and women could only be made to believe in themselves, to realize the powers lying dormant within them, and that all things are possible to the truly awakened and illuminated soul, they would rise above in strength and wisdom. Strive to outgrow the errors of the past; strive to have more faith in the power of truth, honour and goodness than in any personal saviour.

If each and every one could become imbued with the fundamental principle of universal unity, a great step would be taken in the reformation of the world, for then no one would wish to meet his brother or sister on the field of battle. Human life would then be held in greater reverence.

When universal unity is recognized in your political world, what a revolution will have been wrought. The schemer, who now by tricks of trade called legitimate business, will then find it impossible to amass millions of dollars while an honest man may toil for a lifetime for a bare subsistence.

Women should ever bless Spiritualism, for it has done more toward breaking down the barriers of sex and opening wider fields of freedom for her than any other "ism" the world has ever known. The wheels of progress will never cease turning until equality shall exist, not only in name, but in all outward manifestations – social, religious and political.

Humility

Truth is more desirable than all else, and should be gladly received from whatever source it may come. But no one should stultify reason and accept as truth anything that is not susceptible of demonstration.

When a medium shall stand before an intelligent audience and discourse for an hour or more, jingling words together like so many pennies in a boy's pocket, and leaving the audience mystified and in doubt; and the whole farce ended with the announcement that Socrates, Plato or some more modern orator has been the "controlling" intelligence, the effect is anything but inspiring. Such mediums need the education and training of a spiritual kindergarten before going out into the world.

The mistaken idea that mediumship was a special gift of God to a favoured few has been the source of much medium worship. So common has been the notion that a medium was a superior being, a sort of oracle whose statements were considered infallible, that many became arrogant, proud and conceited. When the mind becomes disabused of these notions, and all individuals are regarded as having attributes in common, much of the nonsense attached to the discussion of mediumship will cease. Just as there are highly talented poets, musicians, artists, inventors, orators, authors and so on, so also are there mediums. Because Patti can sing divinely, she should not be designated as a special favourite of the Almighty, but rather one whose faculty of song has been cultivated.

Some of the most accomplished mediums the world has ever known have been unconscious instruments. They have unconsciously dwelt in the vestibule of the spiritual world. Its harmonies have been expressed in their deeds of love, and its beauty in lives of devotion to humanity. Such souls may never be designated as spiritual mediums, yet the mantle more surely envelopes them than it does the "wonderful" medium whose tables may be made to dance, or bells rung, or any other phenomena which are considered so desirable.

Debra Skelton

Discretion

During the recent revival meetings in this city, a young woman commenced tearing off her clothing and screaming that she wanted a robe of white. It required the combined efforts of seven to get her conveyed to the hospital. The trouble was that she believed what she had heard preached and, as a natural sequence, lost her reason.

No sensible, right-minded person could believe in a lake of fire and brimstone where the vast majority of the human family were to be eternally tortured. And that is the kind of stuff that thousands of people flock to hear, and think that they are listening to a divinely inspired teacher. Such preaching should not be allowed in the nineteenth century of civilization. It is a lie, and a blasphemy against divine Love and Wisdom.

Friends, Spiritualists, Freethinkers, what can we do to dispel the clouds of ignorance which have settled so darkly over us? How can we break the news of the eternal world where every aspiration shall find fulfillment and progression? Oh, what a contrast between the debasing doctrines of eternal punishment and the ennobling teachings of a future full of promise, of endless growth and unfoldment.

Every Blade of Grass

Spiritualism is universal. It is no respecter of persons, high or low, rich or poor; all come within its encircling arms of love. God has not opened here and there a few small windows through which the radiance of celestial spheres may shine upon a favoured few, leaving the greater portion of humanity sitting in darkness and doubt! The only obstruction to our view is the degree to which our spiritual perceptions have been developed.

The manifestations of the Presence are many and varied. All animate and inanimate things are outward embodiments of the spiritual forces of the universe. In every murmur of the breeze, in every sobbing wave as it breaks upon the shore, is heard the voice of divinity speaking the needed message to the receptive soul. To the one who is carefully observant in the realm of cause and effect, many wonderful spiritual phenomena will be discovered which would be relegated to the world of chance by the thoughtless and unobservant.

It is not necessary to be a seer in order to perceive spiritual forces shaping the destinies of people and nations in unseen ways. It was but the lifting of the lid of a tea kettle by the force from the boiling water within, that revealed to the receptive mind of Watts something of the power and possibilities of steam. We are not always conscious of being guided by unseen powers. Many would scoff at the very suggestion; yet humanity at large represents only the outward effects of the great world of cause and effect acting upon and through it.

History has revealed the fact of spiritual communications having been received by all nations and people on the planet. Whenever an attempt has been made to impart spiritual or scientific truths to mankind, the instruments through whom they have been given have been made the objects of scorn, ridicule, persecution and, in many instances, have been put to death. Yet, there have always been some souls to whom new truths were acceptable and who chose to proclaim them to the world. These have been the great teachers.

The true Spiritualist need not always enter the séance room in order to commune with loved ones. To those who stand upon the threshold of the open door of knowledge, the séance room is only the school room where the alphabet is mastered. To remain lingering would be as unbecoming to the progressive Spiritualist as it would be for the student who wished to master higher mathematics to confine his studies to addition and subtraction.

The voice of the spirit speaks to all, varying only in outward methods of demonstration. It may be a careless word spoken by some friend, and yet prove a message to you sufficient to change the whole current of your life. It may be a song that spoke to you because it voiced the message in a language you could understand. To the spiritually awakened consciousness of man, every blade of grass is a message of love from the great Over Soul.

Gerald Massey

Gerald Massey
1828-1907
British Poet, Author, Activist

Gerald Massey

Eyes Wide Open

A First-Hand Acquaintance

Worship in Work

Eyes Wide Open

Orthodox religion is mainly built up of scaffolding. The ordinary worshipper stands outside and mistakes the scaffolding for the real building and looks upon it as it rises, tier above tier, like so many landing-stages on the upward way to heaven. Orthodox preachers will go on asserting any number of things which their hearers do not believe, only they have heard them repeated so often until the sense is too out-wearied to rebel. They have evolved our respect by means of the whip. And now when the stick and scourge have lost their terrors, it is found that religious reverence has vanished also.

The young are becoming utterly sceptical in most things, disgusted with the ancient object of reverence, an anthropomorphic God. It is said that the children of this generation have no reverence for God or man. But if the reverence was evoked by the stick, and the reign of the stick is over, what are you going to do? It is of no use complaining, and probably it is too late to think of getting a new stick.

There is a spirit within us that wants to see, with our eyes wide open and each for himself, whether the vision be false or true. Nature gave us eyes to see with; it was man who added the blinkers. Neither men, nor women, nor children will much longer bow down to false authority, or believe blindly as they have done…

> The world is waking from its phantom dreams,
> To make out that which is, from that which seems.

People now demand verification. They must see for themselves that which is set forth as the truth. They must learn whether it has the ring of reality.

Put aside the fable and we are face to face with the fact that we have no power to lose our own soul or damn ourselves for all eternity. If we be immortal by nature, continuity is not based on morality, however much we may retard development by limiting our life. Nor is the hereafter a heaven automatically provided to those who have been deluded and cheated and starved out of their life in this world.

Human life will always have its full share of sorrow and suffering. But nothing can be falser than to found a religion on sorrow and suffering. No! It is not in sorrow, but in joy, that we can attain the greatest unconsciousness of self, and live the larger objective life for others. It is true that sorrow and suffering may add a precious seeing to our sight. That which gives the wound may deposit the pearl. But that is because there is a power which can turn all experience to benefit if our life be right in its root-relationship. Sorrow and suffering are but the passing shadows of things mortal, and not the enduring or eternal reality. If nature has one revelation of truth to make more plainly apparent than another, it is that her creature, the human being, is intended for health and happiness here, in this life, and not merely hereafter. Pleasure is the natural accompaniment of our creative and productive activities.

A First-Hand Acquaintance

We are often told that our western civilization is infinitely indebted to Christianity; but the redemption preached for eighteen hundred years has failed to save the world and it must now give way to other workers with other methods. The coming religion must be founded on knowledge. In knowledge we find a common ground of agreement. We need a first-hand acquaintanceship with the facts of nature, not limiting nature to the little we may know of it at present. That which is based upon knowledge need not be the subject of everlasting contention amongst innumerable sects.

As evidence of a future life, one single proof in spiritual manifestation is worth the hearsay revelation of the world. We have found the bridge in nature that crosses the gulf between the dead and the not-dead; the organic and the inorganic, between mind and matter. We know that the so-called dead are living still. We know they can communicate with us and we with them. We know they can establish a rapport with us more rare and potent than we can with each other in the body.

Spiritualism offers the means of establishing a basis for a doctrine of immortality. It reveals a bridge on which we can get an actual foothold for crossing the gulf of death. The Spiritualist makes connection between the two worlds. Indeed, the two worlds are but one. They are not two, any more than a railway runs through one world by day and another world by night. It is but one world after all, with two aspects. The daylight part of it is but half-revealed by day, and the dark side is but half-concealed by night.

These phenomena show us that we have facts in place of faith. Spiritualism opens up to our vision a Power that operates upon us, through us, and makes use of us whether we will or no, whether we are conscious of its presence or not . Our recognition is unnecessary to its existence or operations. Spiritualism shows us how the soul may be fed with a sustenance drawn from the well of life within us, that is penetrated and replenished from eternal springs. And we maintain that these phenomena demonstrate the natural nexus for the continuity of life, and the next step upward in human evolution.

True Spiritualism will turn our attention to this life and help in the work of this world. Spiritualism, as I interpret it, means a new life in the world, and new life is not brought forth without pain and parting. New light and new life come to enrich, and no harm can befall the nature of that which is eternally true. It is only falsehood that fears the transfiguring touch of light.

Worship in Work

There is a cry of womankind now going up in search of God and it behooves all men to know what it does really and rightly mean. The truth is, that women must be monarch of the marriage-bed. The woman has got to take possession of herself. No woman has any right to part

Debra Skelton

with the absolute ownership of her own body. These, and other things just as vital, will become practical as soon as womankind insist that they shall be practised.

What are we going to teach the children? The life we live with them every day is the teaching that tells. Give the children a knowledge of natural law. Teach the children to become the soldiers of duty instead of the slaves of selfish desire. Children have ears like the very spies of nature herself, and eyes that penetrate all subterfuge and pretence. Guide the curiosity of the little ones whilst it is yet innocent. Give them the best material, the soundest method. Let the spirit-world have a chance as a living influence on them and then let them do the rest. The best ideal of all has to be portrayed by the parents in the realities of life at home. When you are not watching, and the children are – that is when the lessons are learned for life.

My coming religion may suggest a coming revolution. I should not wonder if it does. Anyway, we mean to do our own thinking, and to have absolute freedom of thought and expression. We mean to have the national property restored to the people. We mean that the land shall be open to all. We mean to temper the terror of rampant individualism with the principles of co-operation. We mean for woman to have perfect equality with man, social, religious and political, and her fair share in that equity which is of no sex. In short, we intend the redress of wrongs and the righting of inequalities.

We will have a sincerity of life in place of pretended belief, of joy instead of sorrow; a religion of work, rather than worship; a religion of life – life here, life now, as well as the promise of life everlasting.

Horace Leaf

Horace Leaf
1886-1971
British Author, Lecturer
Healer, Medium

Debra Skelton

Horace Leaf

The Art of Praying

Rightful Reverence

Beyond Our Senses

The Art of Praying

Which books have brought the greatest influence through the ages? Histories, dramas, poems, philosophies, scientific works? No. The scriptures of the world: the Vedas, the Upanishads, the Koran, the Bible, to mention only a few. And what parts of those works have had the greatest effect? The prayers. In our moments of sorrow and aspiration, we turn not to the history of the Israelites but to prayers and meditations.

Prayer is one of the greatest forces known to us. According to comparative religionists, there has never been found a human race without religion, and it is impossible to have religion without a belief in a superior power, whether it be a known deity or an unknown one.

The spirit of prayer has left an indelible mark in history. When humans lived in mud huts, they built magnificent temples. Their best energies and genius were expended in worship and prayer. This is one of the anomalies of history; that in the midst of a crude, inartistic social life, we erected masterpieces to God. The temples of the ancients were built of more than stone. They were born from the heart of the human being in communion with its Maker.

Words and prayers may actually have no relationship whatever. It is the motive, the intention that constitutes real prayer. To quote, parrot-like, some formula makes a person not one iota better in the estimation of God. The art of praying is to mean what you say or do. The art of praying consists in deeds and not words. Mere words cannot make the world better, and they may make it worse. Words ruined Athens. Its orators talked the nation to its doom. All truly great characters are doers, and what applies to them applies equally to all.

On one occasion a letter was addressed to Lord Palmerston, when he was Home Secretary, by the Presbytery of Edinburgh. They inquired whether he intended to advise the Queen to order a day of fasting and prayer to be observed in Scotland, in order to supplicate Divine Providence to halt the epidemic of cholera which was affecting the people in 1854. Lord Palmerston replied to the effect that, since the

Debra Skelton

Maker of the Universe had established certain laws of nature for the planet in which we live, and the weal or woe of mankind depended upon the observance or neglect of those laws, the best thing for the people of Scotland to do was to cleanse their cities and towns of filth and overcrowding, and thus give nature a chance. When they had done their utmost for their own safety, it would be time to invoke the blessing of God.

That Home Secretary knew the art of prayer. It applies all round. If you would pray your best, work your best.

Rightful Reverence

The custom of nearly all institutions is to specialize and keep control of affairs in a few hands. In connection with religion, this has invariably developed into priestcraft; a special education and a distinctive mode of dress making the dispensers of spiritual benefits a class apart. Whether rightly or wrongly, the public taste no longer runs that way. Priests are but human after all.

Spiritualism, on the other hand, makes no such distinction between people and the attainment of truth. Mediums, certainly, stand in a sense apart but they can claim no special virtue. Nature has for some unaccountable reason presented them with valuable gifts, but so has she others. Some people have naturally great memories or fine voices. We admire them for it, but do not reverence them. If anything deserves that, it is the Creator and Presenter of those gifts.

Beyond Our Senses

"After death what?" Today an ever increasing number conclude that death means annihilation.

It is natural that intelligent beings should desire to live forever and that they should regard the possibility of extinction with horror. The struggle for existence arises from a much deeper law than the wish for physical life alone.

This world is far too limited for the average person. Each feels him- or herself pressing against the margin of their physical life. There is within something too big for time and space. A thousand facts give evidence of this. The body is weak, frail stuff, so easily broken and torn to rags; but the soul is often resolute and untouched by these disabilities. In the main, it is the body that hinders them. Marcus Aurelius was right when he spoke of man as a "little soul carrying a corpse", for is not the body subject to purely mechanical and biological laws, whilst the consciousness strives to live above them.

We instinctively long for another chance. The circumstances of life are such that the vast majority of men, women and children have little opportunity to develop more than a fraction of their faculties and powers. The individual longs for a better opportunity for self-expression than this world affords. Why shouldn't Socrates, Plato, Galileo, Kepler and Shakespeare, to mention only a few, be permitted in some other state of existence to continue their researches and exercise their powers still to the advantage of the human race?

Then there are the great demands of friendship and love. The degree to which these entwine themselves into the lives of people is too wonderful to be expressed and too well known to require it. They are the two virtues which make life worth living and they are two qualities the complete loss of which would be intolerable.

One of the principal tasks of religion is to give assurance to the mourner that death does not end all, and that there is the possibility of meeting again those who have gone through its gateway. So essential is such a teaching that its absence would destroy any religion, no matter how powerful it may have been. Whoever has stood by the graveside of a loved one will realize how true this is.

Debra Skelton

How is it then that, notwithstanding the naturalness of the hope of survival of bodily death, so many have lost faith in it? It is because some religious authorities rely solely upon tradition, and tradition is confused, indefinite and contradictory. Go to such a minister and he can do no more than affirm his belief in survival. Being ignorant of the nature of the afterworld state, he will either refrain from attempting to describe it or, if he does, he is sure to differ from his colleagues.

Without evidence, all the faith in the world could not prove survival. The fact that we have deep yearnings, hopes and ambitions is no guarantee that they will be fulfilled. Just as we came into the world without being consulted, so may we go out of it into nothingness no matter how we may hate and fear the thought. Is not this the method of reasoning today and is it not perfectly justifiable?

Spiritualism teaches there is no death. Nor is the world of spirits a world of shades; it is indeed a more real world than our own. To the Spiritualist it is a literal truth that spirits walk this earth unseen and unheard by the vast majority of people. No one goes through life uninfluenced by these invisible hosts, who are quite aware of earthly presences. Who are these unseen beings? They are the spirits of the so-called dead. Viewed casually, this seems improbable simply because we are in the habit of regarding things from the point of view of personal experience. What we cannot see or hear or otherwise perceive through our physical senses, we have difficulty in believing exists at all. The principles of science, however, make it not improbable that there may be, even now, passing through us and the earth invisible planets with cities and inhabitants, mountains and oceans, fields, rivers and various forms of life, though we are quite ignorant of the fact.

The Beyond is only beyond our senses.

W.H. Evans

W.H. Evans
1877-unknown
British Philosopher, Journalist
Educator, Humanitarian

Debra Skelton

W.H. Evans

Just For Today

The Me and the Not Me

Life is Not Haphazard

Aspirational Prayer

Creative Life

Just For Today

Alcoholics Anonymous has a leaflet entitled *Just for Today* which is given to any seeking their help. Wisely the organization makes no great demands, such as getting the would-be teetotaller to pledge to give up alcohol forever. At the start, give it up just for today and renew that pledge every day. I need not go into the psychology of it. The success of A.A. is testimony to the soundness of its methods.

The affirmation, just for today, has wider applications. If we get into the spirit of it we shall see how helpful it can be in many other ways.

"I've had a lot of worries in my life," said Mark Twain, "most of which never happened." It is a fact that it is not the actual thing which we may fear will happen that is the trouble, but our attitude towards it.

Few of us can claim to be carefree. The mistake we make is to carry tomorrow's burdens today. It does not mean that the situation looming before us is to be completely ignored. But there is a vast difference between calmly surveying a coming situation and getting panicky about it before the time comes. When we do come face-to-face with a difficulty, look it bravely and quietly in the face. It shrinks and we see it in right proportions, not in the distorted perspective of our imaginations.

And so, just for today is the right spirit in which to meet our difficulties. We can always find strength to bear the actual burdens of today, but we become stricken with fear and doubt if we add the burdens of the future.

Our present state is a rudimentary one. It is the plane in which the Supreme Mind becomes focused in self-conscious human beings who are endowed with great and wondrous powers. If we catch a glimpse of this and at the same time realize our oneness with the Supreme Mind, we shall know ourselves as immortal beings. But immortality is not living forever, as we so often think; it is the power to live just for today, the power that helps us to unfold from within something of the divinity of the Supreme Mind.

Thus from day to day we face our problems, whatever they are, and so it will always be. For however vast and great our experiences may be, we only live from moment to moment. The actual creative point is not in the past, not in the future. It is here and now.

We are not the sons of time but of eternity, endowed with divine powers to create and direct our lives. We need not be the puppets of fate or fortune, as we so often think we are. So if we adjust our lives to the present moment, with just the glance needed to the future to get our perspective right, we shall live more fully.

Tomorrow? Tomorrow never comes, always it is today. We must not be attached to things or thoughts. They must grow out of us. And what we are determines the nature of the thoughts, things and circumstances in which we are placed. But remember, no matter what the circumstances may be, we must meet them just for today – and out of this will grow a lively faith that will support us in all other days to come.

The Me and the Not Me

It is the relationship of things to ourselves that gives them their impor-tance. While science classifies life forms, it is strangely silent about life itself. For some people, life is thought to be a fortuitous collection of atoms, a result of organized matter; yet how the atoms were fortuitously organized, we are not told. Science collects facts; but facts are only materialized truths. It is the spirit which gives life.

To a thinker, physical relationships are only important in that they show spiritual unfoldment. All the phenomena of Spiritualism are but symbols of hidden forces and higher realms of being.

The divine "me" has emerged here for the purpose of learning the laws which govern it. We may tabulate that which makes up the physical envelope called a human being; but who is the individual behind the mask? It may be that the human form is not the real form of the "me", since forms only indicate progress, not finalities. It may simply be the form best suited to this planet. Evolution is a response to a call. The call and response are continuous. The call is from without, the response is from within. Between the "me" and the "not me" there is constant reciprocity. It was, and still is, the divine circulation whereby spiritual health abounds.

The "I" or "Ego" is the divine self that is always seeking expression on the various planes of being. The "not me" is the echo of the "me". The "not me" is but the reflection of the divine self. Hence, we always find in nature just what we look for. The "not me" is environment. The "me" is the divine selfhood which is the true heredity and uses environment to express itself. It is the "I am that I am" of the mystic.

Life is Not Haphazard

Life is not haphazard, a game due to blind forces interacting one with another, casting upon the shores of matter some spots of self-conscious froth. There is, behind all, aim and purpose. The Immanence of the One is expressed throughout the universe. In us, it rises into self-consciousness which can co-operate with the mighty All.

The highest ideals which have flashed across our minds; the loftiest aspirations ever expressed in art, science, literature and religion, are but outshoots of the One in Whom is all that is. The very fact that we can express the purest sentiments, the loftiest ideals and the cleanest emotions is evidence of a greater self beyond our most powerful imaginings.

Aspirational Prayer

In petitionary prayer, the petitioner has a sense of dependence upon some power without. There is rarely any realization that what one should depend upon is not some power outside of oneself, but the power within one's own being. The child loves to look up to its father or mother, who holds for it all that is good in life. And as we are children of the One, such an attitude is normal and right. But children grow up and, by and by, break from the home and launch out to found other homes. Then father and mother cease to be their authorities and can no longer exercise their parental powers as of old.

So it is with humankind. There comes a time when members of the nation, race or group feel stirring within them latent powers which create feelings of independence, and sometimes this leads to grave differences of opinion. Nevertheless the individual is still dependent upon the group for satisfying most of their needs. That dependence can never be broken.

Now, it is right to try and discover what powers one has and also to develop and direct them. But it is unwise to imagine that they are peculiar to oneself. Everyone has the same powers; the difference lies in their mode of expression. One realizes that the way to a fuller spiritual life is not by petitioning God to give that life, but trying to fit oneself to express it. One must strive to be. Prayer then becomes an aspiration to express in one's being all possible spiritual powers.

Here is discovered the need for keeping the sluices of life open at each end, one for inflow and one for outflow, for true spiritual life is only maintained by the free circulation of spiritual power. One has to give in order to receive. And this must be a giving that is impersonal; there must be no thought of self in it. The more self is forgotten the stronger it becomes. And its strength is that of the life of the One, ever flowing through the self; a flow that renews, cleanses and keeps the whole.

In aspirational prayer one seeks to be; one does not clamour to have one's needs supplied, for one knows they are assured. One realizes that no power which is discovered within is for self alone. Those spiritual relationships which bind each to each carry with them responsibilities. Humanity is one; it is one body, and only as the organs of that body obey the principle of service that lies at the root of all biological functions, can it have health. Thus, to have a healthy humanity we need to have healthy human beings.

Ideas that one race is superior to another must be discarded. Fear lies at the root of the world's woes. Because people do not realize their fundamental unity, they make unfair laws thinking that, by doing so, they are protecting their own interests. But time after time it is shown that the people who legislate for their own selfish protection are really committing suicide.

Those who have discovered what true aspirational prayer is know well that it is met by a corresponding inspiration. You cannot reach up to heaven without its bending down to meet you.

Creative Life

In the effort to discover and unfold power, we may fall into the error that we do it alone. It should be remembered that, when our feet are on the path, many things conspire to help. Every hindrance and obstacle has its value. What opposes should, whenever possible, be used not condemned. You may be sure that every hindrance hides a blessing, but everything depends upon how the hindrance is used. If it is faced with quiet confidence, the power to overcome will be revealed.

It is right that we should develop our powers to the utmost, but it is not in the possession of power that our strength lies, only in the use we make of it. One who seeks his own life alone will not find it, much less realize it. Thus it is in others that we shall find ourselves. To enjoy life, we must give it. To enter into the stillness, we must know the zest of action. We must draw together in ourselves the opposites of being. Love and hate do not cancel each other out. When love flows out, if it meets hatred, it embraces it and transmutes it into itself.

It is not enough to be, we must act. Pious aspiration is not enough. If the One aspired to create a universe and did not put the aspirations into action, there would be no universe. Every thought and plan must continually find expression in the world of manifestation. Life is movement.

The main essential for success in all walks of life is perseverance. So many are lacking in the sticking-plaster principle. Their enthusiasm bubbles up and boils over and so the vessel is rapidly emptied. The quiet persistence which comes from real enthusiasm is none too plentiful. Yet all, at last, either here or hereafter, discover this, and then prepare to become the centres of creative life, centres through which the divine power may flow. Centres that are alive in the One are conscious of that aliveness and co-operate with the One in striving for the healing of the nations.

Elizabeth Lowe Watson

*Sincerely Yours,
Elizabeth Lowe Watson*

Elizabeth Lowe Watson
1843-1921
American Poet, Philosopher, Orator
President, California Suffrage Association
Pastor, First Spiritualist Union of San Francisco

Debra Skelton

Elizabeth Lowe Watson

Sacred Matter, Sacred Spirit

Honesty

Your Inheritance

Come Up Higher

Spiritual Poise

Educating the Soul

No Regrets

The Empire Within

Sacred Matter, Sacred Spirit

In our search after truth, Nature is our only infallible authority.

To violate a law of our own being is to bring upon ourselves sorrowful consequences. If we would enjoy the delights that flow from the fountains of life we must adjust ourselves harmoniously to our surroundings and seek Nature's truths. And if we would expand the realm of thought, it is by studying Nature's pages where, on every side, appear visible forms of invisible force.

We would have you understand that we have a great reverence for what mankind calls matter. We know of nothing profane or unclean in all this universe. What we call matter and spirit are ever changing places. The body is the necessary and beautiful comrade of the spirit, without which the spirit would be deprived of half the pleasure which it now experiences through that medium. Indeed, matter and spirit in the last analysis are one and the same in God.

The innermost thought of God sometimes shines forth in heroic action, sublime patience and the desire to grow morally strong. Life in all of its varied manifestations is a unit. We may call it Nature or God, it is one and the same. It stands for this mighty play of Force.

I affirm then, that we are spirits now as much as we ever shall be. This which we call matter is but the medium through which spirit is manifest. You are all visible mediums of an invisible force.

Is there an architectural form in your beautiful city that was not first an impalpable thrill in some brain? Is there in poetry or song, in the arts and sciences, a single demonstration that was not first a thought? Do you not see, my friends, that every act of our lives is a psychical act or proceeds from the realm of soul? That even yon building is held in place by an invisible force? The strength of the granite lies in the invisible force that holds the atoms and molecules together. Any talk about the unreality of the invisible is pure nonsense.

We know we are thinking beings, yet we never saw a thought. If you say you do not know that you have a soul, I reply, you are a Soul. The Soul called for the hand, the eye, the ear that it might acquaint itself with manifestations of spirit through matter.

Honesty

Let us instil a divine life into every word we utter. Let us be real, honest and sincere. Let us cease to tear down; let us cease to hate, and let us believe in one another, and also believe in the divine appointment of our soul to fulfill some mission in this world. Remember, self-trust is the first secret of success.

Your Inheritance

Whosoever you may be, our message to you and the key we give you to unlock the storehouse of happiness, is this: You have not been called without a purpose; and if you do not fit the niche where you are now, if there are calls you have not yet obeyed, nevertheless no work of your hand has been in vain. Every effort of your being is always tending upward.

Our lives are related to the workings of this boundless universe. All of our struggles and disappointments are but the promptings of the Divine, designed to spur us forward. The very necessity of earning your bread means something more than the labour of your hand; it is training for a nobler work by and by. Every effort that you make is a necessity. All this is simply developing the native powers of the soul and fitting each of you for this grander work that waits further on.

Your happiness will never be complete until you know that you are immortal, until you have risen to a full and clear knowledge that you are destined to fill a place for which this life is but a preparation, and that immortality is yours by natural inheritance.

Come Up Higher

The effect of the dissolution of the body is simply to liberate inherent spiritual qualities, readjusting them to new environments and allowing the consciousness to expand eternally.

The spirit world has accomplished much in establishing, through spiritual phenomena, this fact of our immortality. They have accomplished much if they have determined for you this question: "Shall I have further opportunity for growth after I leave the body? Shall I meet with the friends whom I have loved and lost?"

But there is something beyond this in the work of the spirit world and that is, "What does it signify to me as a moral being?" If I go to a séance and I am convinced that a soul whom I loved once in a visible form has survived the change called death, what of that?

I tell you, my friends, that just as primal human gazed on the magnificent phenomena of nature, unimpressed until spiritual perception blossomed and then drank in the beauty, so may you look upon this phenomena; but if you do not go below the surface and find the roots of moral force, the phenomena will fall flat and dead and do you no good. Whosoever clings continuously to them in their physical phase, and is satisfied with that, is like unto the man who will not rise to his manly estate but continues to amuse himself with the toys of childhood.

For I repeat, the physical phenomena of Spiritualism are only the beginning of our spiritual knowledge. They are only the indices of that which is of more importance and will surely follow, and they will be meaningless and worthless to those who see only in them an amusement; who will not go beyond these and listen to the voice that may be heard through them, appealing to us as a deathless soul to come up higher.

The one step higher of which we speak is that step which shall lead every seeker after spiritual truth to the altar of their own life. You who have felt it a necessity to seek some outside medium in order to communicate with your spirit friend – did you ever think how great is the happiness of that friend when he or she is able to meet you at your own fireside; able to touch you, not through some physical sign, but to breathe into your own spirit the message full of consolation and encouragement.

Can you not understand why the spirit world would plead with you to leave the childish toys and enter into the rich possessions of the spirit? It is only by cultivating this sympathy between your self and the spirit that you can be ministered unto in your times of greatest need.

Spiritual Poise

There is no such thing as the supernatural. Everything that we think and feel and see, whether it be on the plane of the physical or spiritual, is in accordance with eternal law.

Sacred books are simply the history of these spiritual experiences. That which the human soul clings to for strength, for guidance, is the psychical experience of some man or woman of ancient times who, in a partial or perfect trance, heard with other than these outward ears a voice that had been hushed by the grave. I affirm that the law which rendered it possible for the ancient prophets to hear spirit voices was as natural, as universal and as unchangeable as the law of gravitation.

To all these bibles, these records of our spiritual experiences, there is something added day by day. None of them shall ever know completion, for the soul is infinite in its possibilities and has eternity in which to unfold them. Every glimpse we get of the life eternal is an added sentence to these sacred books of humanity.

The lack of these manifestations in ages gone by was not because the law did not exist, but that human life is subject to the law of evolution; just as man waited for a mental development capable of high mathematics, so he waited and still waits for the development of psychical powers.

In connection with this development, we see many distortions of the truth. One would naturally suppose that the demonstration of life beyond the grave would be free from all unseemly disturbances. But here, too, the light of spiritual truth, falling through a great variety of mediums, is infinitely refracted and reveals life's distortions as well as its divine graces. Therefore, we have egotism gone to seed in the notion that heroes, poets and master-souls of the past are again with us clothed in common flesh!

Our credulity is drunk on this new wine. In short, we have lost our spiritual equilibrium. We have sat at the feet of inspired eloquence, drinking in every word as infallible. The more we received of super-mundane facts, the more we craved, and this created an adulterated supply. We wanted the impossible; we got a simulation of it.

And now let us ask if nature's method of growth is not, after all, the surest and best? In proportion to the spreading of the tree's roots do its branches extend, keeping the balance true; in proportion to the respect we pay to life's beginnings, will our faculties unfold for the enjoyment of divine ends. According to our need, as we are prepared, ripened in spirit, the vision comes, the voice is heard, the way appears. Slowly but surely.

Spiritual phenomena should not draw our eyes away from this world. On the contrary, they translate for us its hidden meanings. Let us seek humbly, go carefully along this daily lighted way and, above all, deserve to live forever.

Debra Skelton

Educating the Soul

Nature's method of educating the soul is to visit the reaction of the action upon the soul. To suffer the consequence of our acts here in the physical realm gives us knowledge of the nature of the forces by which we are surrounded and with which we have to deal.

Nature's effects are always for education and reform, and never for the satisfaction of any vengeful ire. So should it be with us. Crime should be dealt with in such manner as to bring the criminal to his or her spiritual sense and reveal to them their true relationship to their fellow human being. When someone commits a crime as the result of the organism, they should meet with such restraint as will educate their soul to higher things.

The consequence of our acts we each should suffer. This is legitimate, and by this we learn wisdom and self-government.

No Regrets

He who wastes time in bootless regret is stealing from God's pure treasury. Regret is worse than hardness of heart if it saps our courage, and is useful only as a spur to higher endeavour.

Let the dead leaves of last year lie undisturbed! Nature will take care that they serve some wise purpose. They enrich the ground and are resurrected in eternal changes of life and beauty. So our dead hopes, our vanished dreams, our faded flowers are not without their sacred use. Higher and purer possessions take their places and if we turn not back, but look forward and upward, we shall see a glow of unborn days flushing the ever-widening horizon and, grateful for the past, we shall meet the future without fear, trusting in the immutable good, forever.

The Empire Within

Make yourself that which is greater than all else, a comforter of your kind, a lover of humanity. The greater the lover, the more successful is the life.

When you think of the great individuals of this world, remember that you are as essential as they. There is an empire within your own life. There is an undiscovered country here which has the power, when you have made yourself acquainted with it, to make you feel that you are at-one-ment with the greatest man or woman that ever lived.

PART TWO: MATTERS & MOTIFS

I. Activism & Equality

Equal Rights for All

Victoria Woodhull
1838-1927
American Medium, Publisher, Stock Broker
Activist, Women's Suffrage Advocate
First Female American Presidential Candidate

Slavery, or a condition of servitude, is subjection to the will of others. I make the plain assertion that the women of this country are as subject to men as slaves were to their masters. The extent of the subjection may be less, and its severity milder, but it is a complete subjection nevertheless.

Because I have announced a new party and myself as a candidate for the next Presidency, I am charged with being influenced by ambition! I take this occasion, once and for all time, to state that I have no personal

Debra Skelton

ambition whatever. All that I have done I did because I believed the interests of humanity would be advanced thereby. Had I been ambitious to become the next President I should have proceeded very differently to accomplish it. I did announce myself as a candidate, and this simple fact has done a great work in compelling people to ask: and why not? This service I have rendered women at the expense of any ambition I might have had.

Permit me again to refer to the importance of following up the advantages we have already gained by rapid and decisive blows for complete victory. Let us do this through the courts wherever possible. It is my candid belief that if women will do one-half their duty, men will be compelled to pass such laws as are necessary, one of which is equal political right for all citizens.

Inner Prompting

John Murray as communicated through

J. Murray Spear
1804-1887
American Minister
Social Reformer, Abolitionist

There are persons who are guided by influences which to them are invisible. They do not see the springs of action, yet they act intelligently and perseveringly, and often reach important ends. Noble men and women, moved upon by unseen influences, have gone forth and unselfishly engaged in the labours that have opened before them. They have not always comprehended the great ends for which they

Debra Skelton

were labouring; but they have had internal promptings and by these they have been guided.

These persons have not been comprehended in their times. Frequently their motives have been misjudged and sometimes they have been sadly abused. Occasionally they have been led to the stake or made to mount the scaffold, or have been left to perish in poverty. And yet they have made their mark, leaving impressions which cannot be eradicated.

By their devotion to truth and duty, these persons have become the regenerators of humankind. Long after their deaths, their influence has been felt, and they have become the models of generations succeeding them. A single woman or man may become the instrument of leading countless thousands to lives of goodness and truth.

How great is the responsibility resting upon every individual, in view of the fact that one does not live simply for oneself. And it should also be ever kept in mind that myriads of unseen intelligences are made happier by the harmony and goodness of the humblest individual. How important, then, that each person should act up to his or her highest standard of rectitude. Today the voice of the inspired may not be regarded. Today their example may not be followed. But there will come an hour when their words will be recalled, their deeds imitated, and they will become sources of new inspirations.

Letter to President Lincoln

Robert Dale Owen
1801–1877
Scottish-born American Spiritualist
Social Reformer, Politician

"To the President of the United States;

"Can you look forward to the future of our country and imagine any state of things in which, with slavery still existing, we should be assured of permanent peace? I cannot. We can, constitutionally, eradicate slavery at this time. But if we fail to do this, then we shall have a fugitive slave law in operation when the war is over. Shall the North have sacrificed a hundred thousand lives to come to that at last? Is the old root of

Debra Skelton

bitterness still to remain in the ground, to sprout and bear fruit in the future as it has borne fruit in the past?

"The questions are addressed to you. For upon you and upon your action more than upon any other one thing does the answer depend. You have, at this time, more power than any constitutional monarch in the world. And for such a power, what a responsibility to God and man!

"It is within your power at this very moment not only to consummate an act of enlightened statesmanship but, as the instrument of the Almighty, to restore to freedom a race of men. We may look through ancient and modern history, yet scarce find a sovereign to whom God offered the privilege of bestowing on humanity a blessing so vast.

"Such an offer comes to no human being twice. It is made to you today."

Homes for the Homeless

William Thomas Stead
1849-1912
British Social Reformer, Journalist

The bitter cry of the disinherited has come to be as familiar in the ears of humankind as the dull roar of the streets or as the moaning of the wind through the trees. And so it rises, year in and year out, and we are too busy or too idle, too indifferent or too selfish to spare it a thought. Only now and then, when some clear voice is heard giving utterance to the miseries of humanity, do we pause in the regular routine of our daily duties and shudder as we realize for one brief moment what life means to the inmates of the slums. But one of the grimmest social problems of our time should be sternly faced, not with a view to profitless emotion, but with a view to its solution.

Is it not time? If, after full and exhaustive consideration we come to the conclusion that nothing can be done, so be it. But if, on the contrary, the heart and intellect revolt against the fatalism of despair, then indeed it is high time that the question of homes for the poor is faced in no mere dilettante spirit, but with a resolute determination to make an end of the crying scandal of our age. It is true that that is much easier said than done. Yet it is the one great domestic problem which religion, humanity and statesmanship are imperatively summoned to solve. Even if it should not be successful, is it not high time to make the attempt?

II. Wise Counsel

A "New Age" Again

W.J. Colville
1862-1917
British Medium, Author

What can be the significance of the strange revival of a passion for everything psychical which has taken hold of the people everywhere? The only answer is to be found in the awakening spirit of the times, which insists upon probing mysteries to their inmost.

There are dangers on every hand for the frivolous and the unwary; but all studies are safe for those who make truth itself the supreme object of their quest. We link ourselves psychically with whatever we love most and think about most. We need not go to India or Egypt to receive illumination, for it is not material journeyings but inward receptivity which brings us into contact with all that we truly need to know.

Out of a babel of conflicting voices and a seething medley of conflicting creeds will assuredly come forth, like gold from the alchemist's crucible, the simple universal religion of humanity. The very impossibility of reconciling diametrically opposed beliefs will have the eventual effect of leading all honest truth-seekers to the light within. The more we fail when we attempt to work from without, the sooner we shall learn to harmonize with nature's divine operations and seek to evolve from within.

In all difficulties let us consult the oracle within and we shall increasingly prove the truth of the magnificent saying, "In quietness and confidence shall be your strength."

Choose Knowledge

Arthur Findlay
1883-1964
British Magistrate, Spiritualist Benefactor
Author, Co-founder: *Psychic News*

Ignorance and misery are twin brothers. Knowledge and happiness are likewise related. Ignorance produces intolerance, misery and discontent; knowledge brings love, tolerance and contentment. Ignorance produces fear and breeds cruelty; knowledge cultivates kindness, hope and truth. Ignorance stands for dejection and selfishness; knowledge brings courage, compassion and generosity. We can choose the one or the other.

Debra Skelton

Spiritualism stands for knowledge. Knowledge makes life understood, is indifferent to old age, and turns life from being a mystery into a great reality. Once it is realized that mind never dies, old age is understood as the preparation for a great awakening to a greater and fuller existence than earth-life can ever give. We are never too old to learn, and knowledge, combined with wisdom, brings satisfaction. Once it is accepted that mind never dies, but only changes its environment, then death is understood to be merely a bend in the road of life. Love is the greatest force in the universe. This great force is not severed by death.

All the good and evil in this world are the result of right or wrong thinking. Each person is master of himself or herself. No king or government, no one can make us think other than we wish to think. Our thoughts can give us happiness or unhappiness, and we must choose which to have for ourselves. Each individual mind sits on its own throne. No one can ever dethrone it or make it think and act other than it wishes to think. It is supreme. Failure and disappointment are words we use to denote a state of mind, but we can make them mean nothing to us if we wish to do so.

Let us therefore be followers of the light of knowledge, and be guided by the lamp of reason.

Healing

Harry Edwards
1893-1976
British Healer, Teacher, Author, Medium

Healing is perhaps the greatest gift that can be desired. It is certainly the most spiritual one.

The desire to heal is a natural talent. Generally speaking, all who feel for those who suffer and have the desire to help, possess the healing potential. There are a few people who are termed "natural healers" in the same way that others may be naturally inclined toward music, mathematics, et cetera.

Debra Skelton

Spirit healing is not the prerogative of any religion or race. It is a common heritage for the whole of the human family. It is extensively practised in the lamaseries of Tibet, and every Mohammedan priest evokes the healing aid for his supplicants. The gift of healing is no more a prerequisite of Christianity than of any other religion. There is not one set of healing laws for the Spiritualist and another for the Methodist or Christian Science practitioner. There are general laws that govern healing, just as there are laws that govern every other effect produced in the universe. What is needed is the knowledge of how they may be best invoked and brought into use.

There are two main schools of thought among those who practise spiritual healing. The first belongs to those who think that a healing is a direct dispensation from the Divine Source, overriding the laws of the universe; a direct and personal gift from God to take away disease from Mr. Brown or Mrs. Smith. This theory rests on what is termed healing through faith. The second theory is, accepting the common basis that all things emanate from God and therefore that healing is a divine act, its fulfillment follows the setting in motion of law-governed processes by wiser discarnate minds who are, indeed, agents within the divine plan.

While many spirit healings seem to be miraculous, there is no such thing as a "miracle", implying an effect that occurs without reasoned order. Every change that takes place within the universe, either materially or spiritually, results from the law-governed forces applied to the subject. This is true whether it applies to the stars in their formation and movements, in the germination and decay of life, or in the construction of an atom – nothing takes place by chance. Law-governed forces control the universe and ourselves within it, and so must they also apply to spirit healing.

The first and perhaps the most important lesson the would-be healer must learn is that he or she does not heal. This is perhaps the most common mistake healers make. There is no personal healing technique. It is worth repeating that the operation of healing takes place through the application of spirit forces. The way to operate these is not yet within the scope of human knowledge; therefore, the human instrument is a channel and is not technically responsible for the healing result. It is an understandable human weakness to desire to be the source of the healing, or to possess the technique or knowledge of how to administer it. It cannot be overemphasized that the healer is not responsible for the healing. One is only the instrument through which it may take place.

It is because we do not yet understand the processes of the healing forces that we cannot foretell what a healing result may be. Therefore, it is not within the power of the human instrument to indicate the outcome to a patient in advance. Neither must we, at any time, limit the power of the healing forces. On occasions, patients have come to the healer with such distressing conditions that the healer's first thought is, "Surely nothing can be done here." To our surprise and amazement, healings have taken place with seemingly impossible cases; yet in the same healing session, an apparently simple disharmony has not yielded to the healing as might be expected.

Healing is directly related to the divine scheme. In the Spiritualist movement it is considered the most priceless of all the psychic gifts. The healer's reward is the joy of healing. The feeling of intense gladness that one experiences when a healing has taken place transcends description.

To be used as an instrument for divine healing brings the healer's spirit self into the ascendant. This does not mean we become unnatural and have to forsake the world and its pleasures. On the contrary, it should make us more natural, and happiness and pleasure are part of our nature. To become unnatural is foreign to the spirit purpose.

Finally, perhaps the real motive for healing is not so much the fulfilling of our own desires to help those who are unfortunate, or the act of making the sick well, but to impress upon the human family that we are all spiritual beings. If this were not so, we could not be healed through the power of spirit. We are spiritual beings. We are animated by spirit.

Through the logic behind spirit healing we can convince mankind of the reality of the truth of survival and assure us of our spiritual nature. This will show us the true purpose of life. As we see this, we will order our lives to good purpose and influence that of our fellows. Our existence

Debra Skelton

will then become a preparation for the greater life before us and thereby the negation of the present code based on materialism, of possessions, greed and profit.

Thus, through the power of spirit healing, we touch the soul of mankind, awakening it to the full opportunities of progression in its real sense. It is the conscious bringing of spirit values into life and the spreading of the seeds of spirituality within the souls and minds of those who are helped in their time of need. And this will imbue existence today with a new concept of life and a fresh power that will inspire the whole of the human family.

Duty

Alfred Kitson
1855-1934
British Author
Founder: British Children's Lyceum

Humanity is a whole, of which the individual is a part, just as the members of a family relate to each other. If any of the family fail in the performance of their duty, then the whole vital economy suffers. This is equally true of humanity.

No one can neglect doing his or her duty without the whole being affected. But unlike the vital economy, the individual has not their part allotted out and set to execute it mechanically. They have to learn what is best for the whole through experience. They must form an accurate

Debra Skelton

judgement of what is their relationship to mankind and therefore what is their duty.

Duty, then, is the performance towards the whole, that which our highest conception dictates as our relation thereto. Insofar as we live up to this, we are doing our duty. The performance of this is the noblest feature of the soul.

Law of Progress

John C. Leonard

The law of progress is one of the grandest truths of all Spiritualism. Other philosophies, of course, teach the law of progress in some form, but Spiritualism regards the law of progress as a definite and actual law in the universe, a law which invariably moves all things to further stations of development and perfection. This law of progress is simply an expression of the will and purpose of God.

The law of progress is universal and is contained in the very structure of all organisms as their inherent creative activity and soul. Every organism and every person, therefore, is bound to progress, for progression is simply the working out and accomplishment of its inherent purpose and destiny. Every organism in nature, according to Plato and according to Spiritualism, is the embodiment, the active creative centre of divine force, ever seeking to give external expression to its inner creative energy and purpose.

Debra Skelton

With respect to human beings this law has its demonstration in those human beings who, having lived on earth and died, have passed on to the spirit world. The earth life was the elementary life, the kindergarten of human experience and the next stage was the spheres of the spirit world. Here the law of progress and development is still operative.

It is necessary that the seed should germinate and bring forth the perfected plant, because all this was contained in an ideal form in the seed. The perfected plant is simply the expression of the purposeful forces contained in the seed. In the same way, it is necessary for the human soul to grow and expand and to develop its latent potentialities because, in doing this, it is giving expression to the intelligent forces inherent in it. The Divine Mind has endowed all organisms in nature with the necessary creative power to bring to fulfilment the purpose inherent in them. There is no exception in the case of the human soul. Like all other organisms in nature, therefore, the human soul must ever progress until it unfolds all the divine attributes and potentialities inherent within it.

III. Modern Revelation

Those Who Dare

Hannen Swaffer
1879-1962
British Drama Critic, Journalist

I am in religion a Spiritualist and a Socialist.

I can see behind all things a Force for good, one that uses us for the working out of its beneficent purpose. I do not expect it to do my work for me. I know that I must do the work myself. I believe that Spiritualism and Socialism will abolish all credal differences, end all class and caste hatreds, join us all in one great human family and build up a new world in which the only distinctions will be the degree of our service to the general good. Believing this, I know that war is the worst of human crimes; I seek to help end all that greedy competition,

Debra Skelton

selfish ambition and economic inequality which make humans strive against each other instead of realizing that they are here, not for self, but for service.

I believe that the kingdom of heaven on earth will be realized when we understand that there is already more than enough for all, that the bounty of Nature is overflowing; and that only selfishness and criminal stupidity stop one from breaking down the wall which, erected by oneself, now stands between us and that kingdom.

Some seek to break down that wall. Some want to climb over it. Some have pierced a small hole and are looking furtively through. But anyway, the wall is there and heaven on earth is on the other side. It is not a dream. It is more than a dream. It is a human possibility.

I know that I make, in the course of my life, an infinity of mistakes. But I do believe that, with all my shortcomings, I am part of a great Plan – a Plan which is working towards that new world and its fulfilment.

Spiritualism is a religion which does not just make statements. It does not rely on a book, or a legend, or what happened in some far-off day, a time concerning which the records are either incomplete or lost altogether. It is something which is demonstrable to any person who, brave enough to throw overboard the false teaching of the ages – truth once, but distorted since by the course of time – dares to stare at the glory of the sun with unblinking eyes.

Such are my beliefs, such my theme.

The Way I See It

Frank T. Blake
1875-1941
British Minister, Healer, Inspirational Speaker

Now the simple truth is that Spiritualism is only a name given to a natural phenomenon of nature. Like the word "physical," it pertains to all that which comes within the range of our physical senses, but with this difference: it connotes all those things which, though not evidenced in physical matter, may be registered by the mind. The word Spiritualism, therefore, is not a word denoting something that is separate and apart from all things else. It is really only a word coined to denote a natural process in nature. In that sense it differs from all religious designations in common use the world over.

Spiritualism is to man what the telescope or the microscope is to the scientist; it reveals what otherwise would remain obscure. It introduces us to hitherto unknown but quite natural phenomena. To become a Spiritualist is to become a scholar. What use you make of your education is another matter. Spiritualist churches are, or should be, colleges of education where those attending may be instructed in the art of living. If they are less than this, they should be closed.

Our public universities educate men and women whose later interests are widely different. These universities do not attempt the moulding of every student in the likeness of one pattern. So it is with Spiritualism. It offers an education that will fit its students to take up every possible human interest with a truer and deeper knowledge of its importance and value in the eternal scheme of things.

There is no my Spiritualism or your Spiritualism. We are both included in its revelation. We may both see what it reveals, though we may differ as to how to use its revealing. That is a matter of personal application and responsibility. To the one, it may be a guide leading to further cosmic knowledge; to another, a spiritual vision giving evidence to support a religious conviction; to yet another, a consolation in times of distress and mental anguish. Spiritualism is a floodlight making clear what was hitherto unknown.

To Liberate the Soul

Paul Miller
British Healer, Author

Spiritualism is true in peace and in war, in good times and in bad, in the darkness of the night and in the bright light of day. It arises not from any desire of any group of people on this earth to foist a new cult on the world, but because there is a plan in the world of spirit to regenerate our lives. It is not done by magic but by the steady presentation of ideas, sometimes consciously, sometimes in the silence of inspiration, but always at work.

The phenomena of Spiritualism are only a small part of the whole. The method is old because human beings do not change much in their ways. From table tappings to spirit photographs, from the discovery of lost languages to the healing of the sick, this work is done. Yet it is not all, for the greatest part is to set free the mind. That is the great task before which all else is small, dear though it may be to all of us to find again the touch of the hand we loved, and to hear again those accents we enjoyed.

I cannot describe anything as a miracle because there can be no miracles in a world of law and order. What is done is done because force moves at the behest of law, and law can be perceived by intelligence and employed. By becoming devotees of nature's methods, we can imitate her actions, speed them up, vary them and learn of laws within laws, of subtler and subtler forces; until we perceive the great unfolding glory of natural science and learn of the endless range of faculties in the human consciousness, and employ them for beneficent purposes. The depths and heights of that consciousness have not been pierced by anyone.

As we grow, the truth we know pales before the truth we are learning. As we evolve, the world around us is unfolding before our perception. Vision is not all. Perception and awareness are more, for in the realms where the eyes cannot see, the mind can perceive, the soul can imbibe and the spirit can express the life that pulsates through the universe.

It has never been claimed by any rational Spiritualist that a complete philosophy has been formulated that will take the place of independent thinking. That precious gift of the spirit must never be taken from us. It is the one safeguard we have against that terrible affliction of creeds and dogmas. The independent mind is as much a spiritual faculty as clairvoyance, clairaudience or automatic writing. Without the clear action of the well-informed mind, there is no safety in this world. Without the constant action of the mind upon facts, there is no means of testing all the statements made in this world and the next.

The purpose of Spiritualism is mainly to liberate the whole force of the soul that it may be fully expressed in life here or hereafter. It is not the aim that every word that is uttered in the séance room, or every idea received in the silence of the communing mind, should be taken as the perfect statement of an infallible God. From the beginning it has been demonstrated that, in addition to the priceless knowledge of continuing life beyond the grave, there is a band of reasonable men and women who are the chief instruments in giving teaching, providing evidence, and finding and guiding the mediums who are their representatives in this world.

Debra Skelton

Sacred Places

Mary E. Cadwallader
Editor: *The Progressive Thinker* (1910-35)

The interest and affection of mankind has ever been centred in the birthplace of leaders, humanitarian movements and religions.

Modern Spiritualism has emerged as a religion, philosophy and science in one. It is more competent to reveal the destiny of man and to train individual souls for citizenship both on earth and in the spiritual realms, than any revelation vouchsafed to man. As the place of emergence from the unseen to the seen, Hydesville, New York is noteworthy in the minds of all Spiritualists. Nevertheless, we should set aside an over-emphasis upon time and place, and bear in mind that communion between the two worlds can be established at any spot where a yearning, aspiring soul recognizes their need of comfort and instruction.

Of old, a few places have seemed to be sacred. Now all places are potentially sacred, and it is for us to make them so in fact.

A Free Mind

James Robertson
Scottish, 19th and Early 20th Century
Speaker, Author

The man or woman who puts the new wine of spiritual natural facts into the old bottles of myth and tradition will never touch the free spirit which observation gives.

The Rational Spiritualist looks with clear, open eyes at what is presented, not seeking to make it harmonize with some orthodox idea which he does not like to give up. We have to get done with the "word of God" that is in opposition to truth as manifested in nature. Religion is not a set of precepts or a given mode of worship. Spiritualism will never bolster up Christianity, though it can throw much light on what is behind all religions. Jesus is still too potent a figure for the world to look at him rationally.

Debra Skelton

That our earthly deeds affect our future life is what all returning spirits keep telling us. Creeds do not count in the eternal court. It is not what we believe or profess, but what we are. Nothing avails there but the life lived. We have no power to lose our own soul or damn ourselves for all eternity. We are immortal by nature.

We have had a religion without knowledge. Now comes a religion based on a common experience. Human souls come back to us, hence we know that life is progressive. The cable is laid between the two worlds and the communications prove that there are intelligent operators at the other end of the line.

Spiritualists have not, of themselves, lifted any veil. The curtain which hid that other world from view has been drawn aside by the spirits' own hands; we have been asked to look at and consider what has been presented in an earnest and truth-loving spirit. The light which has long struggled to show itself now becomes clearer and the question of immortality is removed from the domain of speculation.

The fight to obtain recognition of this revelation of nature has been a hard and long one. Scientists readily believe all the new discoveries in astronomy, chemistry and biology; but when the more important discovery of a spirit world acting upon the plane of matter is proclaimed and valid evidences offered, we hear of credulity and superstition and want of due observation. Such persons have eyes but see not, and ears but hear not. They are forever learning but never coming nearer to a knowledge of the truth.

I do not forget that many of the things I have seen and heard are not made visible to the sight and hearing of those who read my testimony. But I do say that such evidences as have come to me can be obtained by all who will look for them, patiently and with an open mind.

IV. Sceptics

Enthusiasts and Sceptics

Florence Marryat
1833-1899
British Actress, Author
Lecturer, Teacher

There are two classes of people who have done more harm to the cause of Spiritualism than the testimony of all the scientists has done good, and those are the enthusiasts and the sceptics.

The first believe everything they see or hear. Without giving themselves the trouble to obtain proofs of the genuineness of psychic manifestations, they rush impetuously from one acquaintance to the other, detailing their experience with so much exaggeration that they make the absurdity of it patent to all.

Debra Skelton

The second class to which I allude, the sceptics, have not done so much injury to Spiritualism as the enthusiasts because they are, as a rule, so intensely hard-headed and narrow-minded that they overdo their protestations and render them harmless. The sceptics refuse to believe anything because they have found one thing to be a fraud. If one medium deceives, all the mediums must deceive. If one séance is a failure, none can be successful.

I don't mind a sceptic in Spiritualism. But I do object to someone taking part in a séance with the sole intention of detecting deceit – not when it has happened, but before it has happened; of bringing an argumentative mind full of the idea that they are going to be tricked and humbugged. Such an individual wouldn't do so in a human assembly; why should they expect to be more kindly welcomed by a spiritual one? I have seen an immense deal of courtesy shown under such circumstances to persons whom I should like to have seen kicked downstairs. There was a time when I used to take the trouble to try and convince them, but I have long ceased to do so. It is quite indifferent to me what they believe or don't believe.

And with such minds, even if they were convinced of its possibility, they would probably make no good use of spiritual intercourse....

Tongue in Cheek

Mr. Korretyr
Journalist

A Journalist's Report of Phenomena at Falkenberg, June 1885

"At Falkenberg lately, there has been a great commotion about a ghost performing all manner of remarkable things. One man related,

> 'When I went into the house, a brick of peat jumped off the floor at me. Then a knife jumped off the table and came right at my breast and fell. Then a snuff-box jumped off the table and flew at me and fell on the floor. I began to clear out, and just as I was going out of the door, I got a crack on the back, but I didn't turn around to see what it was. I knew well enough it was the devil, so I made off as fast as I could.'

"The very intelligent editor of the great Falkenberg newspaper interested himself in the phenomenon, and discovered that it really was because the old woman had brought home a bone from the churchyard that very probably had belonged to the poor ghost who, dying as a good believing Christian, knew that he would be resurrected by and bye, and that all his bones would be wanted. He couldn't turn up in bits to get a proper sentence. No doubt he will feel an everlasting obligation to the great mind that directs the Falkenberg paper who, in such a masterly manner, discovered the cause of the disturbance and induced the old lady to put the part back in the churchyard whence it had been taken.

"As to table-rapping, the men who call themselves 'doctors' in Stockholm have discovered it to be involuntary muscular action. This muscular action, they mention, is very dangerous because it turns to cramp of a serious nature. If this explanation were true, I have seen tables and many other articles suffering from cramp. The peat, the snuff box and knife at Falkenberg, all were probably suffering from cramp; and this kind of cramp no one knows anything about except the Stockholm doctors. I have studied the subject of Spiritualism for thirteen years, but some people know much more about it than I do – without studying. They are inspired, I suppose."

Just in Case

Minot Savage
1841-1918
American Minister, Researcher
Lecturer, Author

Though I find this life very sweet, I do want another. And though I cannot go so far as to say that this one is not worth having if there *be* no other, I do say that dust and ashes seem a poor and impotent conclusion for such a magnificent, grand, terrible life drama as that we are playing here on this old earth.

No, friends, I expect to keep on. I have no fear of death and I do not regard the grave as my final home. Rather I look upon it as a low arched gateway through which I hope to pass into the sunshine of another life.

Debra Skelton

Meantime, whether we feel assured or not, the best thing we can do is to build ourselves a large and noble life so that, if death does fulfill our hopes and leads us across the threshold of a higher existence, we may be ready to enter it with all the advantage of the best life-training here.

A Fishy Story

Lewis S. Coleman

Once upon a time there lived a man who was very fond of fish – not as an addition to his daily menu, but as companions. So attached was he to the denizens of the deep that he used to row out to sea, don a diving suit and descend to the bed of the ocean every day. So familiar and friendly did he become that the fish used to wait for his arrival and flock round him. He soon learned to converse with them and visited their homes and, except for the drawback of the diving suit, he became almost one of the family.

Then one day, he lost his diving suit and was unable to visit his friends. However, he still went out in his boat and rowed round for hours. But the fish, who could not understand his absence, never came up to the surface to inquire. At last, in despair, he dived into the sea just as he was. The fish saw him and immediately crowded round. But to their indignation, he immediately shot up to the surface again explaining that the conditions were different and he could not stay down there. This did not please the silly fishes, however, who expected him to be as before. So in disgust, they refused to acknowledge him when he would arrive for brief visits among them. At last, a sadder and wiser man, he decided to remain in his own world and leave the foolish fishes to find things out for themselves.

The moral of this will be plain to all Spiritualists. And, as for the others – well, they won't believe in any case.

V. Inspiration

I Feel Within Myself

Victor Hugo
1802-1885
French Poet, Dramatist
Social Reformer, Politician

I feel within myself a future life. I am like a forest which has been cut down several times. The young shoots come again each time stronger, more vigorous. I know I am mounting towards heaven.

Thou sayest that the world is nothing else than the result of material powers. How then can my soul be full of life at the very time when my material force begins to decline? Winter is on my brow, but in my heart there is eternal springtime.

Debra Skelton

In my old age I love to inhale the scent of lilies, violets and roses, just as I did at twenty years of age. The nearer I approach my end, the more distinctly I hear all around me the symphony of the unseen which calls me. It is full of awe, it is marvellous.

For half a century I have put down my thoughts in prose and in verse. I have written about history, about philosophy, drama, novels, tales, satires, odes, songs; I have tried all known paths. But I feel that I have not expressed the thousandth part of what is in me.

Moving towards the grave I can say as many another has said, "My earthly task is finished." But I cannot say, "My life is ended." The tomb is not a blind alley, it is a thoroughfare. It closes on the twilight, it opens on the dawn. I feel refreshed each day because I love the other world as one does his native country. My work is only beginning. I shall rejoice to see it rising up unto eternity.

Make Life Beautiful

Anonymous

Let us do what we can, every one.

It may not be much, externally measured, but estimated by the spirit standard, it is all we have and are, and more could not be asked or expected of us. If we cannot do great things, as they are outwardly measured and weighed, we can each one of us do something. If every life cannot be conspicuous – which is not what it is for – it can at least, and which is better, be beautiful. And the beautiful is the good and true. That only is what we are working for, whether consciously or unconsciously.

We need not think it necessary to work for the applause or praise of others. While our good deeds are not seen, they are all the better for not being corrupted with constant self-consciousness and growing conceit. It is well for us to keep in mind that it is not we who do these worthy deeds, but the spirit within that is continually inspiring.

Debra Skelton

Divinity and Space

Emanuel Swedenborg
1688-1772
Swedish Scientist, Theologian
Author, Inventor, Visionary

Divinity is not in space. Given the Divine Omnipresence, there is no way a merely physical image can encompass the thought that God is not in space. Only a spiritual image will suffice. Physical images are inadequate because they involve space. They are put together out of earthly things, and there is something spatial about every earthly thing we see with our eyes.

Spiritual concepts have nothing to do with space. They have to do solely with state, state being an attribute of love, wisdom, life, desires and the delights they provide – in general, an attribute of what is good and true. A truly spiritual concept of these realities has nothing in common with space.

However, there may seem to be space in the spiritual world where spirits are. Still, it is not space but an appearance of space. It is not fixed and invariant like ours. It can be lengthened and shortened, changed and altered.

With merely earthly concepts we cannot grasp the fact that Divinity is everywhere and still not in space. Spirits understand this quite clearly. This means that we, too, could understand if we would only let a little spiritual light into our thinking. The reason we can understand, is that it is not our bodies that think, but our spirits.

Debra Skelton

The Soul

Cora V. Hatch Richmond
1840-1923
American Medium, Inspirational Speaker
Co-founder: National Spiritualist Association

It is possible for one to conceive that there is a state of perfect happiness, yet no one on earth has ever yet experienced it. It is possible for one to conceive of perfect truth, yet no one should claim to have received it. The infinite cannot be comprehended but can be conceived of by the soul, which is the source, is being, is like God. And this conception can no more be destroyed than the light of day can be destroyed by an intervening cloud.

It is often said that an infinite deity is inconceivable. An infinite deity is incomprehensible, we admit, but not inconceivable. Whatever be the title or designation of that Infinite Being, God is only known within the soul, and only understood in its innermost and divine conception. That is what we mean by the name, God.

This infinite consciousness, or Love, is the prototype for the soul. The soul has its being in eternity, but has its existence and expression in the universe. The soul has to do with all kinds of expressions in time and eternity, but they must be subject to limitations; while God is all in all, now and forevermore.

The soul is related to God, as the finite to the infinite, the resemblance being in quality but not in scope.

To use an illustration, which is not to be taken literally but relatively, the quality of the drop of water is the same as the quality of water in the whole ocean. But the drop will never become the ocean. Even though it seems to be lost in the ocean, its entity as a globule is the same. Or as you are encompassed by the walls of this room, and pervaded by its atmosphere, you are neither the room nor the atmosphere. The finite and the infinite are not interchangeable. Therefore, the soul never becomes infinite, nor is it lost in the infinite. There is no beginning to, nor can there be any cessation of, its being. The soul is finite. Its being must forever be encompassed by the infinite.

The power of understanding this relation is innate to the soul of a human being, and no other basis is possible. When you endeavour to consider Deity by any other method except that which belongs to the soul, there is failure. It is from the soul that there is the first conception of God, the recognition of God, and satisfaction with the consciousness of the presence of God.

Debra Skelton

Wings

Anonymous

We fear to trust our wings. We plume and flutter, but dare not throw our weight upon them. We cling too often to the perch, and excuse our timidity by saying that we are chained to circumstances. Yet there is the great buoyant atmosphere enfolding us, and we are provided with strong spiritual pinions fitting us to float in it. Courage is all we lack....

> *"Be like the bird that, pausing in its flight*
> *Awhile, on bough too light,*
> *Feels it give way beneath it, and yet sings,*
> *Knowing that it hath wings."*

Victor Hugo

PART THREE: VOICES IN VERSE

The Arrow and the Song

Henry Wadsworth Longfellow

I shot an arrow into the air,
It fell to earth, I knew not where;
For, so swiftly it flew, the sight
Could not follow it in its flight.

I breathed a song into the air,
It fell to earth, I knew not where;
For who has sight so keen and strong,
That it can follow the flight of song?

Long, long afterward, in an oak
I found the arrow, still unbroke;
And the song, from beginning to end,
I found again in the heart of a friend.

The Heart Learns

Adelaide Love

The heart learns most of its wisdom when it grieves.
Then it comes to possess
A new attentiveness
And listens for a Word
Not heard
In the tumult of happiness. It leaves
The world for a little while and rests apart,
The sorrowing heart,
And in this solitude
Where none intrude
Perceives
The one immutable design of years;

Debra Skelton

And in the unaccustomed stillness hears
A music which it has not known –
Life's deepest implacable undertone.

As You Go Through Life

Ella Wheeler Wilcox

Don't look for the flaws as you go through life;
And even when you find them,
It is wise and kind to be somewhat blind
And look for the virtue behind them.
For the cloudiest night has a hint of light
Somewhere in its shadows hiding;
It is better by far to hunt for a star,
Than the spots on the sun abiding.

The current of life runs ever away
To the bosom of God's great ocean.
Don't set your force 'gainst the river's course
And think to alter its motion.
Don't waste a curse on the universe –
Remember it lived before you.
Don't butt at the storm with your puny form,
But bend and let it go o'er you.

The world will never adjust itself
To suit your whims to the letter.
Some things must go wrong your whole life long,
And the sooner you know it the better.
It is folly to fight with the Infinite,
And go under at last in the wrestle;
The wiser man shapes into God's plan
As water shapes into a vessel.

I Shall Know Her There

J.M. Peebles

I shall know her there, I shall know her there,
By the shining folds of her wavy hair,
By her faultless form with its airy grace
That an angel's pen might fail to trace –
By the holy smile her lips will wear,
When we meet above, I shall know her there!

I shall know her there, and her calm, dark eyes
Will look in mine with glad surprise,
When my barque, wild-tossed o'er life's rough main,
The far-off port of heaven shall gain;
Though an angel's robe and a crown she wear,
By the song she sings, I shall know her there.

A Medium's Happiest Hour

Mattie E. Hull

When we lead some sorrowing mortal
Upward toward the heavenly portal
*   'Till uplifted is the shadow*
*   From the soul forevermore;*
When we bring the loved to meet you,
And can messages repeat you,
*   Filled with all their love and meaning,*
*   This, the medium's happiest hour.*

Debra Skelton

If Only We Understood

Anonymous

Could we but draw back the curtains
That surround each other's lives,
See the naked heart and spirit,
Know what spur the action gives,
Often we would find it better,
Purer than we judge we should;
We should love each other better
If we only understood.

If we knew the cares and trials,
Knew the efforts all in vain,
And the bitter disappointment,
Understood the loss and gain –
Would the grim, eternal roughness
Seem – I wonder – just the same?
Should we help where now we hinder?
Should we pity where now we blame?

Ah, we judge each other harshly,
Knowing not life's hidden force;
Knowing not the fount of action
Is less turbid at its source:
Seeing not amid the evil
All the golden grains of good:
Oh, we'd love each other better.
If we only understood.

Tubbenden Lane

Rev. G. Vale Owen

You'll be knowing that house in Tubbenden Lane –
Don't know our house in Tubbenden Lane?
Why, it stands on the right, you can see it plain.
There's a strawberry field across the way,
And beyond are the woods where the rabbits play
And the picnickers go of a summer's day.
    It ain't what you'd call a grand domain –
    But you'll see if you go down Tubbenden Lane…

It's the house where me and my missus bides;
There's our bonny darter there besides;
And the boys! Why, they'd make you hold your sides
When they pay us a call, as their work permits;
And the ragging and joking and all, it's – it's –
Well, I can't find the rhyme as exactly fits.
    But that doesn't matter; the thing, in the main,
    Is the love, in the house in Tubbenden Lane.

And there's one more thing as you ought to know;
It's a place where the angels come and go.
No, it ain't very big – it's distinctly small –
But they come in their hosts, and it holds 'em all.
They give us their love, and a blessing too,
Then away they go, for they've much to do.

And I says to the missus, "Old lass, you see
They ain't forgot us." "No dear," says she:
And she weeps while she smiles, as a woman can.
I just let out a cough, me being a man.
Then we turn to and put up a bit of an hymn,
Just to tell the dear Lord as we're grateful to Him,
    For sending His friends from His Grand Domain
    To our own little house in Tubbenden Lane.

Debra Skelton

The Workers Win

Lizzie Doten

The seed which lies inert and cold
Will neither flower nor fruitage bear,
Unless it struggles through the mould
      For light and air.
The soul that seeks for Freedom's prize
Must Freedom's battle first begin –
True effort never vainly dies.
      The workers win.

Through weary years of want and woe
The soul irresolute must wait,
While he who strikes the timely blow
      Will conquer fate.
The might that nerves the hero's arm
Springs from the manly might within;
The coward only flies from harm.
      The workers win.

Oh, fainting soul, take heart of grace,
Though dangers in thy pathway lie,
Pursue thine heaven-appointed ways
      With courage high.
One grand eternal law controls
The life without, the life within.
Heaven is no place for idle souls –
      The workers win.

The Other Man

Anonymous

Perhaps he sometimes slipped a bit –
Well, so have you.
Perhaps he may have faltered –
Why, all men do, and so have I.
You must admit, unless you lie,
That so have you.

Perhaps if we would stop and think
Both I and you,
When painting someone black as ink
As some folks do,
Perhaps if we could recollect,
Perfection we would not expect;
But just a man halfway correct
Like me and you.

I'm just a man who's fairly good,
I'm just like you.
But thankfully I've sense to see
The rest of men with charity;
They're good enough if good as we –
Just men like you.

God's World is Worthy of Better Men

Gerald Massey

Behold! an idle tale they tell,
*   But who shall blame their telling it?*
The rogues have got their cant to sell,
*   The world pays well for selling it!*

Debra Skelton

They say our earth's a desert drear,
       Still plagued with Egypt's blindness!
That we were sent to suffer here,
       And by a God of kindness!

That since the world hath gone astray
       It must be so for ever,
And we should stand still, and obey
       Its Desolators. Never!

We'll labour for the better time,
       With all our might of Press and Pen;
Believe me, 'tis a truth sublime,
       God's world is worthy of better men.

'Twas meant to be, since it began,
       A world of love and gladness:
Its beauty may be marred by man
       With all his crime and madness,

Yet 'tis a fair world still. Love brings
       A sunshine for the dreary;
With all our strife, sweet rest hath wings
       To fold about the weary.

Prepare to die? Prepare to live!
       We know not what is living:
And let us for the world's good give,
       As God is ever giving.

Give Action, Thought, Love, Wealth and Time;
       Work hand and brain, wield Press and Pen:
Believe me, 'tis a truth sublime,
       God's world is worthy of better men.

A Dream

Anonymous

I dreamt death came the other night
And heaven's gate swung wide;
With kindly grace an angel came
To usher me inside.

Yet there to my astonishment
Stood folks I'd known on earth,
Some I had judged as quite unfit
Or of but little worth.

Indignant words rose to my lips
But never were set free;
For every face showed stunned surprise —
No one expected me!

Beyond

Ella Wheeler Wilcox

It seemeth such a little way to me
Across to that strange country – the Beyond;
And yet, not strange, for it has grown to be
The home of those of whom I am so fond;
They make it seem familiar and most dear,
As journeying friends bring distant regions near.

So close it lies, that when my sight is clear
I think I almost see the gleaming strand.
I know I feel those who have gone from here
Come near enough sometimes, to touch my hand.

Debra Skelton

I often think, but for our veiled eyes,
We should find heaven right round about us lies.

I cannot make it seem a day to dread,
When from this dear earth I shall journey out
To that still dearer country of the dead,
And join the lost ones, so long dreamed about.
I love this world, yet shall I love to go
And meet the friends who wait for me, I know.

And so for me there is no sting to death,
And so the grave has lost its victory.
It is but crossing – with a bated breath,
And white, set face – a little strip of sea,
To find the loved ones waiting on the shore,
More beautiful, more precious than before.

What Then?

W.B. Yeats

His chosen comrades thought at school
He must grow a famous man;
He thought the same and lived by rule,
All his twenties crammed with toil;
'What then?' sang Plato's ghost. 'What then?'

Everything he wrote was read,
After certain years he won
Sufficient money for his need,
Friends that have been friends indeed;
'What then?' sang Plato's ghost. 'What then?'

All his happier dreams came true –
A small old house, wife, daughter, son,
Grounds where plum and cabbage grew,

Poets and Wits about him drew;
'What then?' sang Plato's ghost. 'What then?'

'The work is done,' grown old he thought,
'According to my boyish plan;
Let the fools rage, I swerved in naught,
Something to perfection brought';
But louder sang that ghost, 'What then?'

Good Deeds

Alice Carey

True worth is in being, not seeming;
In doing each day that goes by
Some little good thing – not in dreaming
Of great things to do by and by.
For whatever men say in their blindness,
And in spite of their fancies in youth,
There is nothing so kingly as kindness,
And nothing so royal as truth.

We get back our mete as we measure,
We can do no wrong and feel right,
Nor can we give pain and feel pleasure,
For justice avenges each slight.
The air for the wing of the sparrow,
The bush for the robin or wren;
But always the path that is narrow
And straight for the children of men.

We cannot make bargains for blisses,
Nor catch them like fishes in nets;
And sometimes the thing our life misses
Helps more than the thing that it gets;

Debra Skelton

For good lieth not in pursuing,
Nor gaining of great or of small;
But just in doing and doing
As we would be done by, is all.

A Psalm of Life

Henry Wadsworth Longfellow

Tell me not, in mournful numbers,
        Life is but an empty dream!
For the soul is dead that slumbers,
        And things are not what they seem.

Life is real! Life is earnest!
        And the grave is not its goal;
Dust thou art, to dust returnest,
        Was not spoken of the soul.

Not enjoyment, and not sorrow,
        Is our destined end or way;
But to act, that each to-morrow
        Find us farther than to-day.

Art is long, and Time is fleeting,
        And our hearts, though stout and brave,
Still, like muffled drums, are beating
        Funeral marches to the grave.

In the world's broad field of battle,
        In the bivouac of Life,
Be not like dumb, driven cattle!
        Be a hero in the strife!

Trust no Future, howe'er pleasant!
        Let the dead Past bury its dead!

Act – act in the living Present!
Heart within, and God o'erhead!

Lives of great men all remind us
We can make our lives sublime,
And, departing, leave behind us
Footprints on the sands of time;

Footprints, that perhaps another,
Sailing o'er life's solemn main,
A forlorn and shipwrecked brother,
Seeing, shall take heart again.

Let us, then, be up and doing,
With a heart for any fate;
Still achieving, still pursuing,
Learn to labour and to wait.

The House at the End of the Road

Nellie R. White

It is ever so fine just to be glad to live
In a house by the side of the road,
And to be a good friend to the wayfaring man
As he journeys along with his load.

But to me there is something that seems quite as fine;
Let us make it a part of Life's code
Just to speak, now and then, with the wayfaring man
Of the house at the end of the road.

Does he know, and do we, just as much as we might
Of that other, and greater abode
Which is waiting for us when earth's highway shall end,
That new house at the end of the road?

Debra Skelton

And that house, it is builded of timbers we send;
All our thoughts and our deeds make a load
That is daily sent there, by our acts and our prayers,
For a house at the end of the road.

So, then let us send timbers of unselfish love
To be put into that new abode,
And send thoughts of blest peace and of joy to help build
That new house at the end of the road.

We shall find in a garden right next to that house
All the fruit of the seeds that we sowed
As we walked here below with so seldom a thought
Of the house at the end of the road.

So, I'm asking myself some grave questions right now –
Am I building a worthy abode?
Am I proud of the home that's awaiting my soul
In the house at the end of my road?

Jubilate

Lizzie Doten

The world hath felt a quickening breath
From heaven's eternal shore,
And souls triumphant over death
Return to earth once more.
For this we hold our jubilee,
For this with joy we sing –
0 Grave, where is thy victory?
0 Death, where is thy sting?

Our cypress wreaths are laid aside
For amaranthine flowers,
For death's cold wave does not divide

The souls we love, from ours.
From pain and death and sorrow free,
They join with us to sing –
0 Grave, where is thy victory?
0 Death, where is thy sting?

My Neighbour

Nettie Colburn Maynard

Who comes my weary life to bless,
With thoughts and acts of kindliness,
For one who lies in sad duress?
My neighbour.

Who never wished to know my creed,
But only sought to know my need,
And proved they were a friend indeed?
My neighbour.

When crushed and weak with weary pain,
Or bowed by sorrow's bitter rain,
Who comes to cheer me up again?
My neighbour.

Through three long years of helplessness,
Who can their kindness e're express?
I can but ask that God may bless
My neighbour.

If I Knew You and You Knew Me

Nixon Waterman

If I knew you and you knew me –
If both of us could clearly see,
And with an inner sight divine
The meaning of your heart and mine –
I'm sure that we would differ less
And clasp our hands in friendliness;
Our thoughts would pleasantly agree
If I knew you and you knew me.

If I knew you and you knew me,
As each one knows his own self, we
Could look each other in the face
And see therein a truer grace.
Life has so many hidden woes,
So many thorns for every rose;
The "why" of things our hearts would see,
If I knew you and you knew me.

Don't

Anonymous

Don't complain about the weather
For easier 'tis, you'll find,
To make your mind to weather
Than weather to your mind.

Don't complain about the sermon,
And show your lack of wit,
For, like a boot, a sermon hurts
The closer it doth fit.

Don't complain about your neighbour;
For in your neighbour's view
His neighbour is not faultless –
That neighbour being you.

The Clock of Life

Anonymous

The Clock of Life is wound but once,
And no man has the power
To tell just when the hands will stop
At late or early hour.
Now is the only time you own,
Live, love, toil with a will,
Place no faith in tomorrow for
The Clock may then be still.

Debra Skelton

Thank you for listening to the Echoes of the Past.
May they inspire your Present.
Debra

THE END

Vocatus Atque Non Vocatus, Deus Aderit.

About Debra Skelton

Debra Skelton is a healing medium and tutor with the Inner Quest Foundation where she teaches *Sacred Theatre: Dance of the Medium*. She holds a BFA in Theatre from the University of Alberta and studied corporal mime with Etienne Decroux in Paris. She subsequently enjoyed a distinguished career spanning thirty years as a physical theatre actress, choreographer and teacher. Debra is a member of the Open Door Sanctuary in Victoria, Canada, for whom she recorded the popular podcast series and is also, as she says, "an author in service to the Spirit, whatever that may look like and wherever it may lead."

About the Inner Quest Foundation

The Inner Quest Foundation is devoted to the ethical and esoteric development of those pursuing the intuitive arts. Its purpose is to facilitate an awareness of our natural spiritual foundations within the practices of healing mediumship, personal transformation and many of the lesser known aspects of the esoteric experience.

The Inner Quest Foundation also provides an ongoing program of study for the serious student and is host to several international retreats. The Inner Quest has established a worldwide reputation for developing sound spiritual practitioners, fostering creativity within our "everyday mediumship", and reigniting the intrinsically sacred nature of the intuitive arts. It also houses the Inner Quest Press which has published this and other books.

The Inner Quest Foundation is based in Victoria, Canada. Founders Brian Robertson and Simon James have long been sharing their unique esoteric knowledge at major venues around the world by means of public demonstrations, private consultations, television, film, lectures and courses. Within every facet of their extensive practice is to be found a profound dedication to serve all who seek a path to spiritual unfoldment.

We invite you to discover more about the Inner Quest Foundation by visiting our website.

Inner Quest Foundation

Sources

Anonymous, 1896. "Make Life Beautiful" from *Banner of Light*, Boston, MA.

_____. 1932. "Wings" from National Spiritualist Journal, UK.

_____. ND. "A Dream", Source Unknown.

_____. ND. "Don't", Source Unknown.

_____. ND. "If Only We Understood", Source Unknown.

_____. ND. "The Clock of Life", Source Unknown. Note: this poem has been attributed to Wilfred Grindle Conary, Robert H. Smith and others. The version reprinted here was found in a copy of the journal, *Medium and Daybreak*.

_____. ND. "The Other Man", Source Unknown.

Barbanell, M. 1959. "Miracles" from *This is Spiritualism*, Herbert Jenkins Ltd., London, UK.

_____. 1959. "Modern Revelation" from *This is Spiritualism*, Herbert Jenkins Ltd., London, UK.

_____. 1959. "Spiritual United Nations" from *This is Spiritualism*, Herbert Jenkins Ltd., London, UK.

Blake, F. 1934. "The Way I See It" from *What is This Spiritualism?*, Light, London, UK.

Cadwallader, Mary E. 1917. "Sacred Places" from *Hydesville in History*, Progressive Thinker Publishing House, Chicago, IL.

Carey, A. ND. "Good Deeds".

Coleman, L. 1924. "A Fishy Story" from *An Unusual Fishy Story,* The Two Worlds Publishing Company, Manchester, UK.

Colville, W.J. 1900. "A New Age Again" from *Fate Mastered, Destiny Fulfilled*, R.F. Fenno and Company, NY, NY.

Davis, A.J. 1852. "Truth" from *The Great Harmonia*, Benjamin B. Mussey and Co., Boston, MA.
_____. 1852. "A Truthful Mind" from *The Great Harmonia*, Benjamin B. Mussey and Co., Boston, MA.

Doten, L. ND. "The Workers Win".
_____. ND. "Jubilate".

Edwards, H. 1974. "Healing" from *A Guide to the Understanding and Practice of Spiritual Healing*, The Healer Publishing Company Limited, Bromley, Kent, UK.

Evans, W.H. 1925. "Aspirational Prayer" from *Spiritualism: A Philosophy of Life*, Two Worlds Publishing Company, Manchester, UK.
_____. 1925. "Creative Life" from *Spiritualism: A Philosophy of Life,* Two Worlds Publishing Company, Manchester, UK.
_____. 1925. "Life is Not Haphazard" from *Spiritualism: A Philosophy of Life*, Two Worlds Publishing Company, Manchester, UK.
_____. 1925. "The Me and the Not Me" from *Spiritualism: A Philosophy of Life*, Two Worlds Publishing Company, Manchester, UK.
_____. 1953. "Just for Today", Two Worlds Publishing Company, Manchester, UK.

Findlay, A. 1935. "Choose Knowledge" from *The Unfolding Universe*, Spiritualists' National Union, Stansted, UK.

Ford, W. 1993. 1993. "Natural Philosophy" from *The Seeing Eye, The Feeling Heart*, Longdunn Press Ltd., Bristol, UK; by permission of Linda Muir.
_____. 1993. "Spinners of Gold" from *The Seeing Eye, The Feeling Heart*, Longdunn Press Ltd., Bristol, UK; by permission of Linda Muir.
_____. 1993. "The Bigger Picture" from *The Seeing Eye, The Feeling Heart*, Longdunn Press Ltd., Bristol, UK; by permission of Linda Muir.

Hardinge Britten, E. 1860. "Nature of Your Spirit" from *Six Lectures on Theology and Nature*, Self-published, Chicago, IL.
_____. 1866. "Mourning" from Lecture: *The Winter Soirees*, The Spiritual Magazine, London, UK.

_____. 1868. "Seven Sabbaths" from *Second Annual Report of the Glasgow Association. of Spiritualists,* Glasgow, SCT.

_____. 1872 "Footprints of the Pioneers" from preface to *The Spiritual Pilgrim* by J.O. Barrett, William White & Company, Boston, MA.

_____. c1885. "What It Is and What It Is Not" from *Spiritualism: What It Is, And What It Is Not,* Unpublished Private Collection, London, UK.

_____. 1898. "I am Introduced" from *The Grand Spiritual Jubilee,* Two Worlds Publishing Company, Manchester, UK.

Higginson, G. 1993. "Listening" from *On the Side of Angels* by Jean Bassett, Spiritualists' National Union, Stansted, UK.

_____. 1993. "Not Just For The Few" from *On the Side of Angels* by Jean Bassett, Spiritualists' National Union, Stansted, UK.

Hugo, V. c.1890. "I Feel Within Myself" from *A Future Life.*

Hull, M.E. ND. "A Medium's Happiest Hour".

Kitson, A. 1886. "Duty", from *Medium and Daybreak,* London, UK.

Korretyr. 1885. "Tongue In Cheek", from *Medium and Daybreak,* London, UK.

Leaf, H. 1917. "The Art of Praying", from *International Psychic Gazette,* London, UK.

_____.1919. "Beyond Our Senses" from *What Is This Spiritualism?,* Geo. H. Doran Company, NY, NY.

_____. 1919. "Rightful Reverence" from *What Is This Spiritualism?,* Geo. H. Doran Company, NY, NY.

Leonard, J. 1927. "Law of Progress" from *The Higher Spiritualism,* Frederick H. Hitchcock, NY, NY.

Longfellow, H.W. ND. "A Psalm of Life".

_____ ND. "The Arrow and the Song".

Love, A. ND. "The Heart Learns".

Marryat, F. 1891. "Enthusiasts and Sceptics" from *There Is No Death,* National Book Company, NY, NY.

Massey, G. ND. "A First-Hand Acquaintance, Source Unknown.

_____. ND. "Eyes Wide Open".

_____. 1899. "God's World is Worthy of Better Men".

_____. 1899. "Worship In Work" from Lecture: *The Coming Religion*, Self-published, London, UK.

Maynard, N.C. ND. "My Neighbour".

Miller, P. 1976 "To Liberate the Soul" from *The Invisible Presence*, Self-published, UK.

Morse, J.J. 1888. "Duty to this World" from *Practical Occultism*, Carrier Dove Publishing House, San Francisco, CA.

_____. 1888. "Sensible Growth" from *Practical Occultism*, Carrier Dove Publishing House, San Francisco, CA.

_____. 1888. "Special Gifts" from *Practical Occultism*, Carrier Dove Publishing House, San Francisco, CA.

_____. 1888. "The Divinity Within" from *Practical Occultism*, Carrier Dove Publishing House, San Francisco, CA.

_____. 1888. "The Whole Nature" from *Practical Occultism*, Carrier Dove Publishing House, San Francisco, CA.

_____. 1912. "Heart of the Matter" from *Physical Phenomena as a Basis for a Spiritual Religion*, Two Worlds Publishing Company, Manchester, UK.

Owen, G.V. ND. "Tubbenden Lane".

Owen, R.D. 1863. "Letter to President Lincoln, New York 1862" from *The Policy Of Emancipation*, J.B. Lippincott, Philadelphia, PA.

Peebles, J.M. 1872. "At Funerals" from *The Spiritual Pilgrim* by J.O. Barrett, William White & Company, Boston, MA.

_____. 1872. "My Tradition" from *The Spiritual Pilgrim* by J.O. Barrett, William White & Company, Boston, MA, 1872.

_____. 1872. "Refreshing Preaching" from *The Spiritual Pilgrim* by J.O. Barrett, William White & Company, Boston, MA.

_____. 1885. "I Shall Know Her There" from *Medium and Daybreak*, London, UK.

Richmond, C.V.H. 1887. "The Soul" from *The Soul*, The Spiritual Publishing Company, Chicago, IL.

Robertson, J. 1908. "A Free Mind" from *The Open Door,* L.N.Fowler, London, UK.

Savage, M. 1885. "Just in Case" from *Medium and Daybreak,* London, UK.

Schlesinger, J. 1896. "Discretion" from *Workers in the Vineyard,* Self-published, San Francisco, CA.
_____. 1896. "Every Blade of Grass" from *Workers in the Vineyard,* Self-published, San Francisco, CA.
_____. 1896. "Humility" from *Workers in the Vineyard,* Self-published, San Francisco, CA.
_____. 1896. "Work Enough for All" from *Workers in the Vineyard,* Self-published, San Francisco, CA.

Spear, J.M. 1871 "Inner Prompting" from *The Year-Book of Spiritualism for 1871* by H. Tuttle and J.M. Peebles, William White & Company, Boston, MA.

Stead, W.T. 1883. "Homes for the Homeless" from *Pall Mall Gazette,* London, UK.

Swaffer, H. 1945. "Those Who Dare" from *My Greatest Story,* W.H. Allen and Co., London, UK.

Swedenborg, E. 1763. "Divinity and Space" from *Sapientia Angelica de Divino Amore Et de Divina Sapientia,* Amsterdam, NLD.

Tuttle, H. 1878. "A Change Of Sphere" from *The Ethics of Spiritualism: A System of Moral Philosophy, Founded on Evolution and the Continuity of Man's Existence Beyond the Grave,* Religio-Philosophical Publishing House, Chicago, IL.
_____. 1864. "Compassion" from *Arcana of Nature,* W. White & Co., Boston, MA.
_____. 1864. "World Citizens" from *Arcana of Nature,* W. White & Co., Boston, MA.

Wallis, E.W. 1885. "Letter to My Friends" from *Medium and Daybreak,* London, UK.
_____. 1897. "Awakening" from *Lecture at Cavendish Rooms, London for the Marylebone Association of Spiritualists,* Unpublished Private Collection, London, UK.
_____. 1897. "Death's Chiefest Surprise" from *Lecture at Cavendish Rooms, London for the Marylebone Association of Spiritualists,* Unpublished Private Collection, London, UK.

Debra Skelton

_____. 1897 "From Spirit to Spirit" from *Report of a Trance Address by Mr. E.W. Wallis, delivered at Britten Hall, Bridge Street, Manchester, GB*, Two Worlds Publishing Company, Manchester, UK.

Wallis, M.H. and E.W. ND. "Be Thyself" from *A Guide to Mediumship and Psychical Unfoldment*, Office of "Light", London, UK.
_____. ND. "Listen" from *A Guide to Mediumship and Psychical Unfoldment*, Office of "Light", London, UK.
_____. ND. "No Unknowing" from *A Guide to Mediumship and Psychical Unfoldment*, Office of "Light", London, UK.

Waterman, N. ND. "If I Knew You and You Knew Me".

Watson, E.L. 1905. "Come Up Higher" from *Song and Sermon*, Hicks-Judd Company, San Francisco, CA.
_____. 1905 "Educating the Soul" from *Song and Sermon*, Hicks-Judd Company, San Francisco, CA.
_____. 1905. "Honesty" from *Song and Sermon*, Hicks-Judd Company, San Francisco, CA.
_____. 1905. "No Regrets" from *Song and Sermon*, Hicks-Judd Company, San Francisco, CA.
_____. 1905. "Sacred Matter, Sacred Spirit" from *Song and Sermon*, Hicks-Judd Company, San Francisco, CA.
_____. 1905. "Spiritual Poise" from *Song and Sermon*, Hicks-Judd Company, San Francisco, CA.
_____. 1905. "The Empire Within" from *Song and Sermon*, Hicks-Judd Company, San Francisco, CA.
_____. 1905. "Your Inheritance" from *Song and Sermon*, Hicks-Judd Company, San Francisco, CA.

White, N.R. ND. "The House at the End of the Road".

Wilcox, E.W. ND. "As You Go Through Life".
_____. ND. "Beyond".

Woodhull, V. 1871. "Equal Rights For All" from *Speech at Lincoln Hall, Washington, DC*, Self-published, Washington, DC.

Yeats, W.B. ND. "What Then?"